If they could have,

they already would have:
Lessons on Leadership

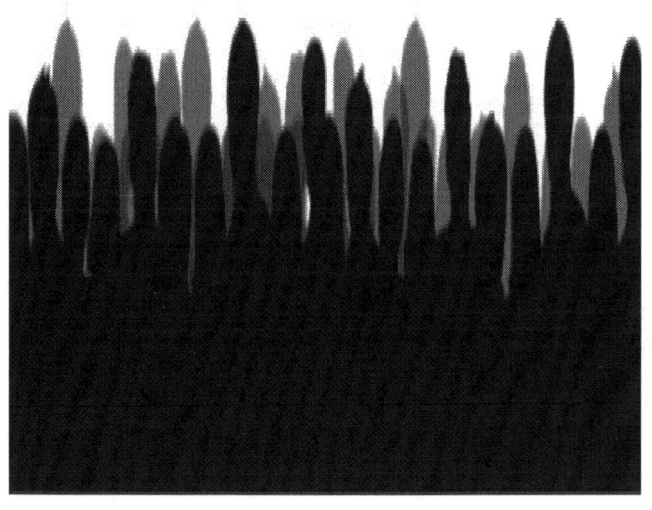

Colonel (Ret) Paula F. Penson
CMSGT (Ret) Jolene R. Meyer

If they could have, they already would have

DEDICATIONS

This book is dedicated to all the superstars hiding in plain sight. We call them our 'SHIPS' and have learned more from them than we could ever hope to teach.

Conversely, we have to thank all of the 'terrible' bosses we have known for they too have taught us more than we could ever have dreamed.

Our loving thanks to our families and friends for the unwavering support.

If They Could Have, They Already Would Have: Lessons on Leadership, © 2016, Paula F. Penson and Jolene R. Meyer.

All rights reserved.

Foreword

"If they could have, they already would have."

What could this mean? It means that most people want to get up in the morning, go to a job that offers them meaningful work, and be successful each day. I am no longer naïve enough to believe that "all" people want to be successful. I now know after four decades in the "work world" and as a supervisor that there are some people who want to stir things up and create chaos. They have grown up in chaos and their "norm" is chaos. They are only comfortable in chaos. If we estimate that the number of people who thrive in this uncomfortable environment to be no more than two percent of the work population, that still leaves 98 percent who want to do the right thing. This book honors the 98 percent.

If employees are not being successful, then, something must be missing. That is what the title of this book means. If they could have … i.e. if they had all the resources, training, and time needed … they already would have been successful. They would have done the job correctly, in a timely manner, and in accordance with company standards, while meeting all criteria of success because they wanted to!

There are only three reasons why someone does not do their job successfully.

If they could have, they already would have

They are:

1. Incompetent
2. Incapable
3. Insubordinate

The job of the leader, then, is to find out which one of these categories applies to each employee.

If they are *incompetent* or unable to do the job, the leader must determine what is missing to make them competent. Is it lack of training or knowledge? Is it lack of computer access? Is it lack of time? The burden is on the shoulders of the first line supervisor. This is the person most likely to be able to assess what is going on with the individual's performance and capabilities. A first line supervisor cannot fix some things. They may not have control over budgets, training dollars, or even the time it would take to fix a situation. Those issues have to be elevated up the organizational chart to middle leaders and senior leaders.

If the employee is *incapable*, it is time to find a job that is a better fit for that employee. This is about intellectual and mechanical competence. I will *never* be an accountant, for example; accounting was not programmed into my DNA or personality. Sometimes people do not "fit" the job for which they have been hired. If they have a good attitude and work ethic, it is worth the time and effort to find them another place within the company to use their skill sets.

If they could have, they already would have

If, however, the person is just unwilling to do the job, i.e. insubordinate, then it is time to remove them from the organization. If you have given the employee all the resources, training, and time but they are not willing to do the job, you must fire them. It is not fair to the 98 percent of your employees who are willing and able to do the job to keep the unwilling subordinate on the payroll. Your first line supervisors will spend 80 percent of their time managing these characters. Do the paperwork and counseling required by your Human Resources Office to fire them. Do it quickly and move on. Then hire the replacement based on work ethic, integrity, and competence.

This book prepares the employer, the first line supervisor, middle leader and senior leaders to understand what is going on for each employee and junior leader. You have to determine if they are *incompetent, incapable, or insubordinate.* Then the leader must identify what is missing if they are not successful, but want to be. Because the bottom line is this ... *if they could have, they already would have.*

If they could have, they already would have

Table of Contents

Chapter 1	Foundational Cornerstones of Success	7
Chapter 2	If they could have, they already would have	34
Chapter 3	First Line Supervisors	53
Chapter 4	Outstanding Attracts Outstanding	95
Chapter 5	Improvement & Organization...One Team at a Time	109
Chapter 6	Career Cycles	116
Chapter 7	Senior Leaders	122
Chapter 8	Three Campaigns	155
Chapter 9	Leaders as Problem Solvers	167
Chapter 10	Get Up, Suit Up, and Show Up!	180
Epilogue	Final Lesson: The Show Must Go On!	182
Biographies		186

If they could have, they already would have

Chapter 1

Foundational Cornerstones of Success

The heart of individual success is based on whether or not a particular individual has the foundational cornerstones for success. Does he have a good work ethic, integrity and the willingness to do a good job? Each person must have these characteristics no matter where he sits within the company.

My secrets for success are not secrets at all; they are the foundational cornerstones by which I try to live every aspect of my life. Fortunately, they have also served me very well in my career. I willingly share them. These cornerstones are necessary for each individual to achieve personal greatness and for each organization to maximize company objectives.

These eight cornerstones for individual success are:

1. Visible **competence**
2. Humble **confidence**
3. Personal **accountability**
4. Personal **courage**
5. Undaunted **perseverance**
6. Ability to **lead** from wherever you sit
7. Desire to **serve** something greater than yourself
8. **Get up, suit up, and show up** every day!

If they could have, they already would have

Visible Competence

Visible competence is being the person who others trust to have the knowledge about a particular field of expertise: in other words, to be the 'go-to' person. These people know the laws, rules and regulations, or at least know where to go to find the answers. They stay abreast of changing requirements and can walk anyone through their processes and procedures.

Someone once asked me, "What do you think has been the key to your success?" I thought about it for a few minutes and narrowed it down to two words: visible competence. Having confidence in yourself and your work is one thing, but being visible is as important. The two words, "visible" and "competence" must go together. You might be the smartest Subject Matter Expert (SME) in the world; but if you are hidden in a cubicle someplace and no one is aware that you are a great superstar, what good will it do? How will management ever utilize you? How will someone put you in a position to have an even bigger impact in the organization?

I saw visible competence vividly demonstrated the first time I met my business partner and life-long friend. I was sitting in my first staff meeting as the Administrative Assistant to the Commanding Colonel of a large Air Force Fighter Wing. It was a long and tedious meeting, going over flying missions, aircraft status, personnel manning and training statistics, etc. This two-hour meeting concluded with the commander going around the room asking everyone if they had anything else to add or bring up. After about 30 people had been asked and most had no comments, and all were glassy-eyed with information overload, the Colonel circled around to the Master Sergeant sitting next to me. I did not know who she was or what job she had, but it was obvious that the others did. The demeanor of the room changed immediately. People re-engaged and actually grabbed pens to take notes as she rattled off her business for the meeting. She spoke clearly and precisely and when questioned, answered in such a way that you knew the information was correct and factual. I had never witnessed so obvious an example of visible competence before. I knew then that I wanted to get to know this person. She is the co-author of this book and we have been best friends ever since.

There are many superstars in the world, hiding in plain sight! We, the leadership -- specifically the first-line supervisor--have first "eyes on" and the responsibility to identify these superstars-in-the-making.

We have to identify these people, and then provide opportunities for them to succeed. It is best to start them off on a lower level project as the Program Manager, and then move them up to a larger, more complex project. They are learning and gaining competence as they work their way up the ladder of difficulty and complexity. They learn how to identify the requirements and the resources they will need, how to put together a schedule or planning tool, how to divide, conquer, and delegate, and how to backwards plan and use other program management tools that will enable their success. It is important that you start

If they could have, they already would have

them out slowly, building their confidence and competence along the way.

Early in my career, I had a boss that did that for me. We were moving into a new building space vacated by others, and the layout was not suited to our mission. Even though I was one of the lowest-ranking members of the staff and had no experience with renovations, my boss assigned me as the point of contact (POC) of this huge project. With little or no direction, he told me to figure out how we should best use the space. His lack of direction was not a lack of caring; he was placing no boundaries on my efforts and creativity.

This was evident when I showed him my draft plan. I began with, "I know it is grandiose. The engineers probably will not support it or it will cost too much ..." He stopped me mid-sentence and said, "Never be your own worst enemy! Always shoot for the stars and then settle for the moon if you have to." That was a very valuable lesson. I dug in and learned what I needed to learn and the plan came off almost as originally designed. I was hugely successful through visible competence. I gained confidence in my own capabilities and others gained confidence in me. It was a tipping point in my career.

Humble Confidence

The second cornerstone of success is **humble confidence**. I emphasis the word *humble* as there is a fine line--no, make that a big fat dark line--between being cocky and being humbly confident. Having the maturity to recognize the difference is imperative to success.

Humble confidence is being able to be the go-to person without the know-it-all syndrome attached. You are internally confident in your abilities and do not need to tell the world how good you are. You are polished in your ability to share your knowledge and expertise in an unassuming manner. You do not need the world to know you are in the room, that is a given. I learned this lesson from a fellow student in my Master's program at Arizona State University. She quietly said to me, "You can't learn anything new, if you're doing all the talking." She was politely trying to tell me to shut up and listen! She was also reminding me that being a know-it-all was not impressing anyone.

Additionally, we have to ensure our actions and our words match. A favorite quote of mine is from <u>Social Aims</u> by Ralph Waldo Emerson, published in 1875. He said, *"Be still, for what you are stands over you and speaks so loudly I cannot hear what you say."* Our actions tell on us every day. Make sure you are not sending rival messages between your actions and your words. Ensure your confidence is based on facts, historical evidence of success, solid integrity, and overall competence.

Seek feedback to test your self-perception. If you want to know yourself, let someone else tell you a few truths. Allow someone you trust to put an honest mirror in front of you. You may find the results very interesting. It is a

If they could have, they already would have

sign of maturity first to seek and then to listen to feedback. It is a sign of courage to act on it.

I had a significant epiphany that helped me to look at myself honestly for the first time. I was seeing a family counselor, discussing concerns I was having with my children's behavior. My counselor said to me, "If you change yourself, your children will change!" I realized that my children were reacting to my behaviors. It is both exhilarating and scary when you see yourself in your children's behaviors. It makes you stop and think about the impact you have on those young minds, and on other people around you.

The key aspect to humble confidence is humility. I learned it was not all about me when dealing with my clients' needs versus my own needs as a consultant. As a person that spent more nights a year in a hotel bed than in my own, it would be very easy for me to slip into believing and acting as though it were all about me. A client's request to change a meeting time or place could send me scurrying for cover. "This schedule was previously approved and coordinated with all concerned!" oozed through my thoughts. The comment, "If I move your appointment then it will cause a problem for someone else," might slip out as I tried guilt as a means to avoid having the headache of making scheduling changes. As I felt this defensiveness creeping in, I had to stop myself and remember the "ME" rule, and realize that my humility was lacking. It is not about me; it is about providing my clients a service. There always will be legitimate and not-so-legitimate reasons for clients to change appointments. I can still provide that service if I stop and remember that my job is not about me–it is to "**E**" my clients and students. It is to Enlighten, to Entertain, to Empower, to Enrich, and to Engage. If I pressure them to stick to the established schedule, I probably will have clients and students that dis-engage or are dis-enchanted, and then who wins? I may have won that battle; but in the end, I provided a disservice to all. Our job as leaders is to "**E**" our employees: Enlighten, Entertain, Empower, Enrich, and Engage.

Personal Accountability

Living with **personal accountability** is the hardest to maintain and sustain under peer pressure. As we know, one "ahh sh-t" can wipe out a hundred "atta-boys" in one moment of weakness. Holding yourself accountable for your actions is crucial. No one else should ever have to hold you accountable if you hold yourself accountable first!

To be trustworthy *you must be worthy of trust.* Your actions and behaviors have to say to others that you are worthy of their trust. You must prove this day-by-day with your every action and word. Your word must be your bond. If you lose your credibility, it is hard to get it back.

I had a possible breaking point with my own credibility within our Air Force Fighter Wing. I had to muster all the personal courage I could find inside myself to do the right thing. We were having a large-scale war-fighting insppection in which we were simulating being under a chemical agent attack. My role was to be the technical

If they could have, they already would have

advisor to the commander in the Survival Recovery Center (SRC). This center consisted of experts from each recovery area such as civil engineers, medical personnel, communication experts, and me, the so-called expert on nuclear, chemical and biological warfare actions. The tensions were high and the tempo frantic as we tried to recover our base after a simulated chemical attack wearing full chemical protective gear. If you have never had the opportunity to wear this gear, imagine being encased in a broiler oven fashioned as a suit of clothing. Every exposed inch of your body is covered by rubber or a charcoal-lined material. Nothing breathes. You are drenched in sweat and have to work with clumsy gloves on. Your speech is garbled and the visibility through the mask is dismal at best, but you can function and you can survive.

My nine reconnaissance teams were out in the field at various locations on the base testing for chemical agents. Once they all radioed in negative chemical reports, the SRC commander would be able to lower our response posture, declare an "All clear" for chemical exposure, and we would be able to take off our protective suits and go back to working in our normal battle gear. That "All clear" was my goal. It was extremely hard for anyone to function in the gear and we needed to get out of it as quickly as possible. I remember seeing all the beady eyes of my fellow SRC members watching me through their gas masks and hearing the muffled roar of the Colonel in the Battle Staff room hollering for status on the chemical tests. The pressure was on…all base personnel had been wearing their gas masks and full protective gear for hours. Heat

If they could have, they already would have

exhaustion was becoming a real concern. Heat stroke could become a real-world result if this went on much longer.

The chemical test results take time and a negative report is required from each sector before the safety of the Airmen on the entire base can be assured. Only after hearing a negative from all sectors could I recommend to the SRC commander to stand down our posture. Eight teams had radioed a negative report and there was one team left. I reported to the SRC Commander, "Sir, eight were negative; one more to go."

All you could hear was the labored exhalations from the gas masks as everyone in the room stood poised to strip off their masks and pass the all-clear to the field. What was taking that last team so long?

Finally the radio squawked and we heard the team chief report, "Venom One, this is Venom Nine."

I grabbed the mike and squeezed the button. "Go ahead, Venom Nine."

"Venom Nine ready to transmit a type three report. Are you ready to copy?" said the distorted voice talking through the gas mask.

"Go ahead, Venom Nine, Venom One, ready to copy."

A series of numbers were rattled off as I filled in my report sheet that translated to the results of the chemical test. I intuitively knew what the results were going to be. The

15

If they could have, they already would have

Inspector General (IG) team had kept us in chemical gear for an unprecedented amount of time and this had to be the all-clear we were waiting for.

Well, my assumptions were never more wrong. In my haste, and with my poor assumptions guiding me, I transposed the results on the report sheet and declared to the commander that we were all clear. As the notices went out to the field, and people were gleefully stripping off their gear, the frantic Venom Nine team chief tried to break in on the radio traffic to inform me of my mistake. By the time he did, it was too late. Everyone was out of gear and was at risk.

In the aftermath of the war game, the IG's preliminary evaluation of the situation was that the Venom Nine team reported the results incorrectly, and that I had responded correctly to the data I was given. The exercise was a success and the inexperienced Venom Nine team excused for their simple mistake. Overall, we expected to receive an "Outstanding" rating, the highest grade possible for the exercise. It was time for the party to begin.

I did not feel like celebrating. It would have been so easy to gloss this over and let it ride. In fact, for the benefit of the Wing, it was better to let it go. But could I do that? I sought out the IG member who had been with the Venom Nine team and assembled that team. Together we pieced together the mistake that I had made. He told us that in the heat of the exercise it was not clear to anyone but us who had made the mistake, and that we should just let it go.

If they could have, they already would have

He said, "The team performed admirably and the overall results were great." As I looked at my team it was obvious to me I could not let it go. They had done their job; they did it well and they did it right. *I* was the one who had messed up their report and reported a negative when it should have been "inconclusive, retest required."

The IG member said, "All you did was jump the gun by ten minutes. I was going to provide a negative report after the next test was run anyway. No harm, no foul."

The Venom Nine team, composed of mid-level Airmen, was willing to take one for the team and support me, their team chief. We looked like heroes to the Wing, so why rock the boat? But could I really allow this to happen? Why did I need to come clean? I had admitted my error to the team and their dignity was intact. The IG had moved on, so why could I not do the same? If the IG chose to change our grade because this error was at a command level and not a first-line technician level, the results for the Wing could be detrimental. To say I was conflicted would be an understatement. It was obvious to me that the reputation of my team and my integrity were all that mattered.

It did not take long to set up an appointment with the Colonel who was the Wing Commander and the Colonel who was the inspection team chief since they were both in the Colonel's office patting each other on the back for the successful war-gaming efforts. With all the military bearing I could muster, I spilled the beans on the last crucial step of our recovery action. A pin could have been

If they could have, they already would have

heard dropping as both of these officers listened to my confession.

The Team Chief countered with the fact, "It was still a very successful training activity. Mistakes are made by everyone, and that is why we do training." My Commander instead asked me a question, "Why did you feel the need to bring this to us, as it is obviously not a concern to anyone but you?" I swallowed and replied, "Sir, if this would have been real-world and not an exercise, my actions could have resulted in injuring or killing my fellow Airmen. That mistake is something that I cannot take lightly. As it was, it was just a training environment, an environment where we ask every one of our Airmen to do their part to ensure that we all survive and recover after an attack. My Venom Nine recon team did their job, did it well with the pressure of an inspector watching them, and while wearing full protective gear. On the other hand, my performance was less than perfect. I know that as humans, we will never be perfect and I am able to live with that. What I am unable to live with is allowing my team to take the rap for me. I want them to trust me; I need them to trust me because if there is ever a real-world attack, how could they know I am worthy of their trust if I am able to bury this issue?"

My statement was not making it easy for my superiors to respond. It was water under the bridge by now…the inspection had terminated hours before and the out-brief was scheduled for early the next morning. I apologized for my error, asked them to consider my recon team's performance and left. I agonized that night while waiting

If they could have, they already would have

for the briefing the next morning. Not because I had screwed up; I could live with that. It was the fact that my desire to come clean would probably affect my whole organization and bring our overall score down. We were expecting to get an overall "Outstanding." Was my moral code of self-righteousness important enough to affect a 1,200-person Wing? I was very surprised that the reporting of the error did not give me that cleansing, "You did the right thing" feeling. Instead, I felt like throwing up as I carried the weight of the Wing on my conscience.

As I entered the auditorium the next day, greeted as a hero, the positive energy in the room was staggering. Everyone was ecstatic, knowing we had nailed the hardest inspection we were ever likely to undergo. I was devastated to realize that I could very easily be the catalyst for our downfall. Was my team going to be happier knowing their tiny piece of the puzzle was done right? Many people approached me with glad tidings and asked what was wrong with me, as my demeanor was less than jubilant. I spouted off jokingly, "I miss wearing the gas mask."

In the end, the overall grade for the Wing was still an "Outstanding" and the Venom recon teams received an "Outstanding." The SRC was dropped from "Outstanding" to an "Excellent." Not many people knew the true reason why the SRC grade was changed. For those who did know, half of them told me I had been a fool for bringing it up, and the other half said they would have expected no less from me. The Wing moved on to the next mission, but I still to this day remember vividly the day my choices were bigger than myself.

If they could have, they already would have

Personal accountability was illustrated in yet another situation. It taught me that right was not always right; it is your motivation that counts. A colleague of mine, John, was tasked to set up a roundtable meeting where people were to meet with a visiting VIP. He set up the meeting for the following week and had a core group of people who agreed to attend. The day of the meeting, which he was not scheduled to attend, he received a call from his boss asking, "Where is everyone?"

The meeting was scheduled to start but the roundtable looked more like an arc table because only about half of the scheduled attendees had shown up. In frustration, John started calling the participants' supervisors to see about quickly filling the room. I overheard one conversation that bothered me. John spoke to one of the supervisors, Pete, who in turn raised one of the missing employees, Bill, on the radio. Pete asked Bill why he was not at the meeting as we listened in.

In an instant, you could tell by the sound of Bill's voice that he had totally forgotten about the meeting. Bill replied, "I remember John mentioning it but he didn't tell me the time or place. I am working in the field now and there is not enough time for me to make it back for the meeting." John immediately went on the defensive and relayed the message, "I remember watching you write the appointment down in your planner."

Pete soon terminated the radio conversation when it was apparent that it was deteriorating into a "he said/he said"

If they could have, they already would have

flail. He told Bill, "I will talk to you when you get back at the end of the day."

John was outraged and frustrated that Bill had obviously lied. The conversation between Pete and John continued to bounce the situation back and forth. The core values of the company centered on honesty and integrity. John felt strongly that Bill was not living those values and should be held accountable for his actions. John vehemently stated, "This is not about Bill missing the meeting; it is about him not taking personal responsibility and being dishonest." Pete listened and sympathized with John but basically excused Bill, saying that Bill had been real busy and he was sure that it was not deliberate.

As the conversation wore on, I started to doubt John's motives. Was John right that Bill had lied and not met his commitment? Probably. Was John justified in thinking that he had done his job in setting up the meeting and Bill had dropped the ball? Probably. The problem was that the underlying tone I sensed from John was that it was not really about the values of honesty and integrity at all. It was more important for John's ego to see Bill disciplined because John had been made to look bad in front of the VIP. He was using the company values as a sword. The fact still remained that the round table did not have all the participants and hours were spent on massaging someone's heart instead of really fixing the problem.

If they could have, they already would have

We must always hold ourselves to the highest possible standards, especially when in a leadership role. You have to evaluate your motives and your actions continually. You cannot expect your subordinates to perform at the highest standards if you are not doing so yourself. You should never, ever have to be held accountable by someone else. You should take care of that responsibility yourself.

Personal Courage

Personal courage is tested continuously throughout a career. There are decision points at which you will have to take a stand and do what is right, even when it is not popular to do so. Ignoring or glossing over a breach of integrity, even if you are not guilty of it, sends a silent message to others that you condone it, since you are doing nothing about it. Sometimes, you have to have the personal courage to do the right thing even when no one else around you is doing so.

It is not enough for you to know what is right and wrong; sometimes you must take the appropriate action to ensure that the right thing is done. You may even have to give your own supervisor some tough, honest feedback. As a leader, your responsibility is to keep everyone in compliance, whether that is a supervisor, a peer or your subordinates.

As a Technical Sergeant (mid-level technician) in charge of a large organization-wide program supporting our operational readiness inspection response, I once learned a valuable lesson about lip service. The program required

If they could have, they already would have

participation by all 1,200 personnel. It was not well received but it was understood to be unavoidable if we were to pass the inspection. My mandatory training took the Airmen away from doing their "real" jobs. I took that concern into consideration when I developed a training plan that was endorsed by the executive steering committee. I left that meeting delighted knowing that I had the support I needed for participation by 1,200 personnel.

How wrong I was! I found out the definition of lip service firsthand. It started with my co-workers in the hallway asking if I could sign them off this one time because they had something else more important to do. The word soon got out that bribery, however charismatically delivered, was not going to work with me. I could not relent and pencil-whip even one of the 1,200 souls. I was afraid that if I gave an inch to one person, it would turn into a mile with others beating a path to my door. This training was crucial to passing the inspection and crucial to obtaining the knowledge they would need in a combat zone. I truly believed their lives could depend on knowing this stuff.

I thought I was over this hurdle because members started to comply and attend the training; however, I had not seen anyone from the largest group in the organization yet. This Group Commander was the type of man you either loved or hated. I normally did not deal directly with him, but I had been on the receiving end of his biting criticism in the past and was a little leery. The people who worked directly for him appeared to like and respect him. Others outside that group described him in a less positive light, so I learned to avoid him as much as possible. He was

If they could have, they already would have

probably the third most powerful leader in the organization and was known for protecting his own people at the expense of others. He would shield them from what he felt were superfluous details that fell beneath their station. It was very rare to see one of his people assigned to a set-up or clean-up detail. They had the reputation of being prima donnas in the organization. I was not surprised when not one of his people had attended the required training.

I was more than a little surprised; however, when I received a call from his secretary saying, "The Colonel wants to see you in his office to discuss an implementation plan." I replied, "I'll see when my supervisor is free and get back to you to confirm the meeting." She said, "I was told to inform you that your supervisor is not needed at this meeting as it's your program; you have all the corporate knowledge needed for this purpose." This was true; however, it was a strange request since this Commander never dealt with underlings if he could avoid it. I agreed to the meeting with more than a little trepidation. I arrived early, looked sharp, and with a smile on my face reported to his secretary with high hopes of developing a successful implementation plan. I was shocked when I was told to go straight into his office.

I found all of his group's Chief Master Sergeants (highest of the enlisted ranks and seen as demigods in the eyes of the enlisted corps) standing up and lining the walls around the room even though there were plenty of chairs at the conference table. I knew them all by sight but not very well. Not one word was uttered by those Chiefs as I was

If they could have, they already would have

instructed by the Colonel to sit in the chair in front of his desk; they all just stood and stared.

This may sound naïve, but this was not the normal way of holding a meeting in our organization. Just the fact that they were all in the room ahead of the scheduled meeting start time was rare and had to be a first in itself. If I had found them all crowded around the table ready to roll up their sleeves and start negotiating, that would have been normal. This was a gauntlet that I had to run before reaching my hot seat in front of the Colonel. Once I was seated, he started informing me how much of an imposition my tasking was with no opening pleasantries, introduction of his staff, or even an acknowledgement of their existence.

This was intimidation, pure and simple; and I was out-numbered and out-maneuvered. With my pulse racing, I realized I had a split second to decide how to deal with this. It was time to run the "OODA Loop" used by fighter pilots flying combat missions: Observe, Orient, Decide, Act – Repeat. As the saying goes in the fighter world, I was "too close for missiles; switching to guns." The bottom line was that this situation had little to do with the planning efforts at hand and more to do with my character as a person. As soon as the Colonel paused for a breath, I interrupted him and stood up.

With all the bearing and courage I could muster, I looked him in the eye and said "Sir, with your permission, I would like to stand as I feel I am being disrespectful to your Chiefs and the rank that they hold." I turned to the Chiefs

If they could have, they already would have

and said, "Gentlemen, with your permission," and I went and stood beside them against the wall and said, "Sir, please continue."

I received a few smirks from the Chiefs and it was very apparent that I had thrown the Colonel off his game. The meeting terminated minutes later with the excuse of another obligation that he had forgotten and a need to reschedule. The next day, the maintenance folks started complying with the original plan and the meeting was never rescheduled.

This is a drastic example of the situations we find ourselves in, and the seconds in which we have to make decisions. I went with my heart, my foundational cornerstone of personal courage and stood by my integrity. I did not get angry—scared, yes; angry, no—even though I would have had every right to be defensive about being set up. I chose not to allow myself to play the game at the Colonel's level. We had many more dealings over the years, and though they were not all pleasant, I had established ground rules that day in his office. Many years later, at my retirement ceremony, I was surprised to see him in the audience. I figured it was probably one of those "your presence will be duly noted by your absence" sort of affairs, so I did not think too much about it. What did surprise me was when he came up to me later, shook my hand and told me, "Chief, you have more integrity and perseverance than anyone I have ever known. I wish I could have been more like you." I was stunned into silence, wished I had a tape recorder, and mumbled my thanks as he walked away.

If they could have, they already would have

Undaunted Perseverance

When I think of undaunted perseverance, I always think of an older gentleman that I used to work with when I first joined the Air Force. He was the type that had an old-fashioned saying for any situation. One of his favorites was "No hill for a stepper". Over thirty years later I heard his words in my head as I entered the "storeroom" which I discovered after I was working in an agency for over six months. I was working as a financial officer in a headquarter-level Air Force organization in the DC area. It was a room, assigned to us in the basement of this huge building, which had been a catchall for years. I was informed there were some financial contracts that belonged to parts of our organization that had been shut down and I should review them. What I found was two complete pallets of banker boxes crammed full of papers that had been abandoned, ignored, or passed on. There had to be at least a hundred unlabeled and unsorted boxes of financial documents and government contracts that had belonged to our organizations that closed. I had an unbelievable task ahead of me. All I heard was "No hill for a stepper" and started to break the task down into manageable steps. First sort by year, they sort by type, then determine if all obligations against contract were complete, then either file or destroy. It sounded much easier when written down in an action plan. My co-workers had been too overwhelmed by the scale of the project to have done anything about it prior and chose not to claim ownership. I could not do that. I owned it the minute I discovered that they were financial documents. A very long story short ... in my spare time, I completed that action plan in a little over a year's time. I left an organized file cabinet with about ten open contracts to monitor. Too bad, I did not have a Fitbit on as I definitely got my daily dose of "steps" with that project.

Long-term perseverance is critical for life-long success. After being fired three times in fifteen years, it would be easy to give up on my dreams. After the third time, I had to look in the mirror and accept that I was the common denominator. It was time to change me. I was living the definition of insanity, i.e. doing the same thing repeatedly and expecting a different result. A new job gave me the skill that eventually changed my entire career path and led to my ultimate success. It was basic problem-solving skills. I became known as the problem-solver. In essence, my focus was to meet or exceed the needs of the organization. I stopped worrying about getting credit or recognition. Amazingly, when you become good at problem solving, rewards and recognition follow. When your motives are pure and you sustain undaunted perseverance, goals are achievable. See chapters nine and ten for more about problem solving and perseverance in action.

Ability to Lead From Wherever You Sit

The most important element of individual success is the willingness to LEAD! America needs leadership now more than ever before. We need leaders with personal courage, competence, confidence, character, innovativeness, and greatness. We need leaders who step up into the vacuum when no one else will.

If they could have, they already would have

It takes personal courage to assume the responsibility and mantle of leadership. You have to be willing to step out front--alone and visible to all--and assume the responsibility to accomplish the mission through others. You have to be willing to take on projects and programs and to figure out how to make everything work toward a common goal. You need to be able to identify problems, and to recognize when you are the problem! You have to be able to identify the needs of the organization, the stakeholders, and the people, then do something about it!

You need to be a whistleblower in the purest sense of the word. Being a yes man to your boss is not doing your organization any good. If all he hears are his own ideas regurgitated back to him, he could have stayed alone in his office and not wasted his time in a meeting.

You have to take personal responsibility to be an effective leader. No sitting on the sidelines looking like a toy puppy in the back window of the car with your head a-bobbin' unless you really do feel that what you heard is the best plan at hand. You sometimes need to take the lead when all others are silent.

At a conference in a roomful of the highest-ranking people, I saw a senior non-commissioned officer (NCO) take the initiative and lead from where he sat. This Chief Master Sergeant spoke up and said, "We do not have anything scheduled for this hour, so we could take a long break or we could use this time to talk about what we can do to develop our members and prepare them for leadership roles." The ensuing discussion was very beneficial and a

If they could have, they already would have

much better use of our time than taking a break. It takes courage to be a risk taker, and to step up in front of other leaders. You take risks when you put your ideas out there for others to shoot down or support.

America's military leaders have to be prime examples of what leadership looks like and accomplishes. They are held to a higher standard and need to step up to that standard. They are expected to be the ultimate standard of leadership for others to emulate. When they fall from grace, it is a big fall!

Leadership can be as simple as making a suggestion or volunteering to do a project. It is as simple as saying, "Ma'am, I have an idea." or "Sir, I think I know a better way to do that." or "Sir, how about if I take that off your hands as a special project?" For example, I went to my commander and asked him for something special to do to position me for my next promotion. He reached into his drawer and pulled out a folder labeled "THTD." It was his "too hard to do" folder. He told me I could work on anything in that folder and that he would be eternally grateful. The simple act of looking for some work to do was a singular act of leadership. (By the way, I finished every project in that folder and was promoted.)

If they could have, they already would have

Desire to Serve Something Greater than Yourself – Every day!

To be successful you will need knowledge, abilities, problem solving and program management skills, and a great work ethic! You have to be willing to work twelve-hour days without being told. You have to be willing to make sacrifices knowing that sometimes your family will suffer. The results will be that you are going to be recognized, you are going to be promoted, and you are going to be given additional roles and responsibilities that set you up for even higher levels of promotion.

You have to tie visible competence and humble confidence to your knowledge, abilities, and skills. You must then be willing to serve something greater than yourself every day, or you are just self-serving. Service needs to become a mindset, and it is not about expecting some kind of reward every time you spend an hour extra to get the mission done.

Always looking for compensation or recognition for every minute that you exert yourself is not going to get you what you want. It is counter-intuitive. The harder you work and the less you seek recognition, the more recognition you will get. Serving something greater than yourself can happen in many ways. None are too big or too small. The size is not important; the act is.

I had the honor of being the guest speaker at a Veteran's Day celebration sponsored by a Veterans of Foreign Wars (VFW) group. In the speech, I talked about the importance

If they could have, they already would have

of serving something greater than yourself. I challenged the audience to find the talent they possessed and share it with others. I challenged them to volunteer with the Boy Scouts or at the local school, a nursing home or charity. It did not matter where, just that they do it.

After the speech was over many members of the audience came up to shake my hand and tell me how I had inspired them. At the end of receiving line, patiently waiting his turn, was a boy of about fifteen with special needs along with his parents.

When it was finally his turn, he grabbed my hand and wildly shook it with a grin plastered on his face that extended from ear-to-ear. He kept saying repeatedly, "My puppets, my puppets!" in a very excited manner. I turned to his parents for an explanation. They smiled and said, "He figured out how he serves something greater than himself. He has puppets that he plays with and he loves to tell stories with them. He entertains his fellow students in his school with his puppet shows."

He replied, "Yep! It makes them smile and the younger kids are not so afraid of school anymore. I serve; right?" I grabbed his hand and shook it and then smartly rendered him a military salute and said, "Why yes, you do! Yes, you do! You are a fine citizen for doing that! You and your parents should be very proud."

That was a defining moment in my own life. An angel touched me that day, housed in the body of a very special boy who clearly understood what it meant to serve

If they could have, they already would have

something greater than himself. He got it! He knew immediately that his puppets were his gift of service to others.

Get up, suit up, and show up each and every day!

This concept is discussed in detail in chapter 10.

Chapter 2

If they could have,
they already would have!

It is easy to believe that most people want to succeed in life...in their jobs, their families, their ventures. Right? They want to do a good job and act intelligently. No one wakes up in the morning, looks in the mirror and says, "I can't wait to be stupid today!" This is true for everyone: employees, first line supervisors, middle managers, all the way to the top!

You may know a couple of people that fall into the exception category, but I will bet 98 percent want to go to work and be successful each day by whatever their definition of success may be! Success to them might be winning an argument against management or joining leadership to achieve a common goal. Most people want to leave work every day feeling as though they have accomplished something of which they can be proud.

Why is it, then, that there seems to be the task or project that your employees never get done? It is probably filed in their "THTD" file. You know, the "To Hard To Do" file that we all have filled with projects that keep getting shuffled lower and lower in the stack. It is crucial to understand the *why* or the project will probably never get done. The person who does not get a project or task done usually falls into one of three categories. The employee is

If they could have, they already would have

one of three things: *incompetent, incapable, or insubordinate.*

These three distinct categories of *incompetent, incapable, or insubordinate* may overlap or intertwine and in some cases masquerade as one of the others. Each must be understood to be able to unlock the true meaning of the others. The insubordinate person is generally the hardest to correct or sort out, but in all three cases it is necessary to peel back the onion to see into which category they fall. The corrective action plan for each category is quite different and not knowing the underlying cause can result in further delays in performance and results in greater frustration for you and the employee.

Incompetent

The most important thing to remember for the category of *incompetent* is that it is not the employee's fault. This is not *incapable.* Some external factor is slowing him down. The *incompetent* person, in this context, is eager, has a great attitude, is intelligent, and wants to do a good job. His lack of accomplishment is a moment in time and not a general characteristic of his behavior.

Incompetence usually stems from a system failure of some sort. It could be that the employee does not have the correct training, or the computer does not work, or does not have the correct software or the individual does not have proper access to a website. There are artificial barriers keeping her from doing the job. It could be that she was provided insufficient guidance on what the task

If they could have, they already would have

was or what was required. This was a leadership systemic failure. The employee was only given enough information, training, and resources to fail.

The *incompetent* employee may be the easiest to figure out, but could end up being the most complex to solve. There could be myriad reasons why a person is not doing what you expected him to do. Maybe he is afraid to say he does not know, and he is wasting time trying to figure it out on his own. It is uncomfortable for many people to admit that they do not know or that they cannot do something. Others may not try at all because they think they are not allowed or are restricted from doing something.

Your first step is to do an assessment. Ask yourself, "What does this person need to be successful or productive? Is the gap in training, knowledge, skills, computers, access to systems, tools (literally and figuratively), mentorship, help, literacy, etc.?"

If it is a system issue, that is generally easy to fix. Depending on what the task or project is the person may not have the access or the information he needs to gain access. Does he need to complete an on-line training course for an office requirement? An example may be that his name keeps appearing on the "bad boy" list for not completing computer security training. Why? Does he know the web site? Is his computer set up with the appropriate supporting files such as flash drives, acrobat readers, speakers, or headphones? Does he know the course title and password? The *incompetent* employee

If they could have, they already would have

situation is usually a system or process problem that, once corrected, enables the task to be completed. Some systems and processes are interdependent. You may have to do extensive analysis to see where the problems are located if it is not obvious at first.

Once you have assessed the gap between employee performance and system-related resources, but you realize there is still something missing (i.e. the employee is still not doing the right thing), you have to look in the mirror, and say, "What am I not doing as a leader/manager/ supervisor? Have I given the employee everything he needs to understand the task?"

Have I led by GRACE?

G	Goals	directions, guidelines, end-in-mind, deliverables, milestones
R	Resources	tools, time, money, people, policies
A	Abilities	skills, project size, check-back points
C	Conse-quences	boundaries, deadlines, rewards
E	Evaluation	feedback

Leading by GRACE is covered in more detail in chapter 3, First Line Supervisors.

The bottom line with *incompetence* is that it generally falls in leadership's court to remove the barriers that stand in the way. Once done, the employee is going to be successful. Peeling back the onion to find which of the three categories applies (*incompetent, incapable, or insubordinate*) to a non-successful employee is required. Can you now eliminate the *incompetent* aspect of the equation? If you can, then the person has the tools to complete the task. If the work is done, then *incompetence* was the only reason for failure or lack of success. If the project or work is still not happening, then it is time to move on and evaluate the other two categories: *incapable* or *insubordinate.*

Incapable

Incapable applies to those cases when there are no limitations on employee performance created by the system. *Incapable* is a job mismatch. A person may have gotten into a job for which she has no natural aptitude, and she will never totally succeed, even though she has a great attitude and is making a good effort. The person just cannot do the job at hand. This is not good for that person, her co-workers, or the organization. It is even more problematic when the person is well-liked. Everyone must be capable of performing work to an established standard. A worker may have other talents, but the skill set required for this particular job is not there now and may not be easy for her to learn. This does not mean that the person does not have value, but you need to find out where her talents lie and do the right thing as a leader and get her into that job. If you truly like the person, find the right fit. You will have a loyal employee for life.

If they could have, they already would have

An obvious mismatch, for example, might be a job requiring physical strength or endurance but it is seriously lacking in a particular worker. Sometimes people do not fit correctly into the job to which they have been assigned. In this case, you have a person who is very willing and excited to do the job, but cannot do the job--it is not that she will not do the job. She should never have been placed into that career field in the first place and her real talent is being wasted. For example, I will never be an accountant. I would fail miserably if I had to depend upon that career field for my livelihood. It is totally the wrong fit for my skills, knowledge, and abilities. I will fail; I am *incapable* of being a successful accountant. I will also never be a brain surgeon, because I cannot stand the sight of blood.

I have seen this mismatch vividly displayed throughout my career and want to share some stories that demonstrate it. When I was on active duty, I worked with a young man, a Technical Sergeant (mid-level technician), who was about to be kicked out of the military for incompetence. This man could not push paper if his life depended on it. He was always trying hard, but frequently felt overwhelmed. Whenever any of the office machinery would break, however, he was the go-to-guy who would fix it. He could make the oldest piece of junk work again. Finally, a Chief Master Sergeant (senior enlisted manager) said, "Let's transfer this guy over to the maintenance organization, since he is so good with his hands."

He ended up going up through all the ranks and did a great job in maintenance. He was just *incapable* in the administrative world. He was mismatched in his career

If they could have, they already would have

field. His natural skills were at complete odds with his assigned career field. He went on to be promoted to Chief Master Sergeant and retired after 33 years from a key role at a headquarters-level command.

The opposite case was true with a Staff Sergeant (mid-level technician). She was assigned as an electrician. She was a nice person and a good worker but the problem was that she could never get over her fear of electricity. She was cross-trained into an administrative position and went on to do very well in her new career field.

The *incapable* aspect of the equation deals with a person's skill set mentally, intellectually, emotionally, and physically. It deals with their levels of experience, maturity, social capacity, and communication skills.

The questions to ask are: Is this person capable of completing the task? Is the project so complex that she cannot see the big picture of what needs to be done? Is she too daunted by the task that she is frozen and cannot progress? When faced with a massive program or project, we learn to "eat the elephant one bite at a time." Is the worker able to do this? If you get a so-called finished project from her but are left wondering where the rest of it is, is she incompetent or *incapable?* Are you asking yourself questions such as: What about the analysis or the proposals? Would it not have been nice to see the metrics and data from which she drew her assumptions?

People without strong project management backgrounds may tend to think in a linear way. They may be able to answer the direct question at hand but not provide leadership with enough data to understand the process or problem. They did not provide enough data to drive a decision. Now you have a completed project that does not meet your needs. You have to ask yourself, was the person *incapable* of this task or was the task given without sufficient guidelines and understanding for her to succeed? Was the person set up to fail in her venture? There is a fine line between what the worker should have known and what we fail to provide. Assumptions on the part of both parties can easily result in the person being *incapable* of succeeding.

In the military, the recruiter often gives each new recruit a list of available jobs, maybe three or four for which he is qualified due to his entrance exam scores. The employee usually makes a choice on a pre-conceived perception of the job title and not what the job entails or the skills he possesses. I talked to a retired Navy friend, and he related his story about his own experience. He was nineteen years old, looking to leave home and break out into the big bad world. The recruiter gave him three choices: cook, aircraft mechanic, and medic since those were the priority career fields needed at the time. As he was pondering his choices, he thought back into his previous life experiences. Cook…no, almost burned down my mom's kitchen when I was a teen because I left bacon unattended on the stove. Mechanic…no, I remember the days of my dad's jabs at me for not knowing the difference between an allen wrench and a crescent wrench. Medic…Hollywood, movies, heroes...the thoughts were starting to form in his grey matter, but alas…his decision was made when the

If they could have, they already would have

recruiter commented that his fellow sailors would call him "Doc." As romantic visions of old war movies played in his head, he saw himself as the man of the hour, responding to his fallen comrades as they rang out their call for "Help, Medic!" So medic it was! In reality he became a Respiratory Therapist and no one ever called him Doc. Even though he was successful, he never really felt that it was what he wanted to do as a career.

I personally decided to be a nurse. From childhood, I remember tending to my dolls and pets and informing anyone who would listen that I was going to be the next Florence Nightingale and heal the world. I was the 1960's version of the Disney Junior series, Doc McStuffins. So off to college I went, studied hard, got my degree, passed the State Boards with the normal degree of anxiety and nail biting and set off on my new career. My innocent twenty-something self was in for a surprise. I was tasked with night shifts for the foreseeable future, doctors who knew they were gods and did not appreciate late night calls from nurses telling them their patient's condition had deteriorated, and worst of all, tons of paperwork. To say the least, I was disillusioned. The time spent with the actual patient care was limited because of my shift and duties. I was not healing the world; I was killing trees. Yes, I was capable, I had the license to prove it, but I was not truly motivated and my passion was dwindling. It only took me a few years to realize that it was time for me to get a new career.

I am not sure that all people can identify their own mismatched status. If they can, do they have the courage

If they could have, they already would have

and know-how to do anything about it? I shocked everyone who knew me when I joined the Air Force, embarking on a totally new career. All I was taking with me was a stack of student loans and a desire to do "something" special with my life.

In other cases of *incapable* employees, it is caused when a person has risen to the level of their incompetence. A person performs well in an organization and keeps being promoted until they are promoted into a job that is beyond their level of ability; i.e. one level above competence.

I remember a perfect example of this from a Master Sergeant. He was the Senior Technician for an Air Force Squadron. His duties required that he oversaw the work of the full-time technicians and kept the squadron functioning between unit training assemblies, the weekend duty where all the guardsmen reported to work. Well, this Sergeant was great at detail work: analyzing records, keeping track of data, etc. He was not great, however, at supervising, overseeing, and directing others. The squadron was afloat without a rudder. Everyone was busy doing things but the direction was unclear and if a project ever came to fruition, it was probably by accident.

It was time for commander intervention. I inherited this staff, and after an observation period, it was obvious to me that we had reached the point of dysfunction. "If they could have…they already would have," was echoing in my mind. What ensued was many counseling session with the Master Sergeant where we developed detailed work performance plans for him. Improvement was shown when

43

If they could have, they already would have

specific tasks or plans were required, but when it came time to pass the baton back and have him run the show, things would slowly revert to chaos. The *incompetent* aspect had been identified. The systems were in place to support productivity but results still did not occur. The "last man standing" rule was in effect (he was *incapable)*. This sergeant did not have, nor was he able to assimilate, the leadership skills required to lead his employees. After all the counseling and performance plans, this realization was not a surprise to him, his subordinates, or me. The senior noncommissioned officer ranks in the military require leadership of others, a trait at which he did not excel. It was time for a change for this mismatched employee and he was relieved of his position.

This is one of a supervisor or commander's hardest tasks. Not only is it gut-wrenching because you are taking away someone's livelihood, it is also plain hard to do within the Federal employment system. There are mountains of paperwork required to pass through all the wickets and legal reviews to ensure that a person is being relieved for cause.

There is a happy ending to this story. Once relieved of his full-time position, he used his educational benefits and attended nursing school. He recently graduated, and became a very *competent* nurse!

Sometimes, however, you may have a person who is *insubordinate* but is hiding under the guise of *incompetent or incapable*. If the job is still not being done and the person has been given all the requisite resources and

If they could have, they already would have

training, and has the inherent talent and skills, then it is time to investigate further and look at the last category. Is he being *insubordinate?*

Insubordinate

The *insubordinate* person provides the most unique dynamic. Is she unwilling to perform, and therefore, is *insubordinate* for one project or task or generally underperforming and unwilling to do her work or be part of the team effort? Is she lazy? It is essential at this point to have eliminated the *incompetent* or *incapable* categories before going further with determining if someone is *insubordinate* and unwilling to perform. Once you feel that *insubordinate* is the correct assessment, i.e. the "last man standing" rule, then you need to dig deeper. Ask yourself what influences may be affecting her by asking questions like those listed below.

- Has the person's behavior recently changed? If so, what has happened to influence the change?
- Is there family or a personal problem going on?
- Are there health issues?
- Has there been a workplace conflict or other workplace event that would influence her?
- Is there a new mix of people in the office?
- Have there been any external influences, such as policy changes?
- What kind of rapport do you have with this person?

Now it is time to determine if the person is genuinely *insubordinate* and unwilling to do the job.

If they could have, they already would have

Are you able to have difficult, but civil, talks with the employee without the conversation deteriorating into defensive mud-slinging? If not, one way to diffuse the emotional conversation is to ask the person to write out a response and get back with you later to discuss it. It is better to do the follow-up later when tempers are in check.

When conducting the interview with the person, it is essential that you hear his words as well as the underlying feelings. Understanding a person's feelings is the starting place to understanding his motivation.

Ask the employee to provide you with a noun that describes how he is feeling. Then ask him to provide you an example by feeding the noun back into a sentence. A few examples are shown.

If they could have, they already would have

When I try to work on _____ (project), I feel _____.

Feeling	Effect	Cause
Over-whelmed	I feel overwhelmed when…it is time to go to the staff meeting and I know I will be spending an hour of my day in a meeting that is pulling me away from the pile of work I have to do that is sitting on my desk.	Problem prioritizing work. Not seeing the benefit of the meeting. Insecure because he may be called to task.
Frustrated	I feel frustrated when…I am sitting at my desk struggling to concentrate on my work and others in the office are spending extensive time reliving last night's sports events over-and-over again.	Does not feel work is evenly distributed. Does not feel others are pulling their weight. May not feel that he fits in with office mates.
Confused	I am so confused when I try to work on the project. I do not know where to start as there are so many moving parts.	Unable to break the project down into workable parts. May not be able to see the big picture.
Used	When I even think of working on the project, I feel I will be wasting my time. No one will read or use the thing when I am done.	Does not understand the overall purpose of the work task and/or how it will benefit the organization.

Motivation and work ethic are other factors you need to examine. As we all know, there comes a time in every workday when you come to the realization that you are not going to accomplish one more productive thing. This is normal and okay for most because they use these last few minutes cleaning up emails or checking on suspense dates.

If they could have, they already would have

It is not okay when the person reaches this stage before lunch and spends the rest of the day watching YouTube videos.

Once you start to narrow down the cause for the lack of productivity, then you can move into the effect it has on the employee. Are any of these influences acceptable justification for not doing the job? In the truest sense, the answer is no. As workers, we are expected to keep our personal life personal and our work life productive. The military joke, "If Uncle Sam would have wanted you to have a family, he would have issued you one," echoes this sentiment. We know that it is not humanly possible or healthy to separate our home and work lives but still the expectation is there to fix it and move on. Sometimes, we as leaders have to be there to provide the extra help needed so workers can move on.

If you resolve all the possible negative influences and the person is still *insubordinate*, then it is a discipline problem and a leadership issue. The person must be brought to task to get inside the boundaries of expectable behavior or suffer the permanent consequences. I normally find that people like this will self-select out when they are brought to task. They will apply for new jobs and go elsewhere as they believe the grass is always greener on the other side.

The problem is that they forget that they take themselves with them. If the problem is their own character and value systems (work ethic, laziness), then it does not matter what color the grass is on the other side. If they were mediocre here, they will be mediocre there. If they were worthless here, they will be worthless there. If they were gossips here, they will be gossips there. At some point, they have to change themselves instead of changing jobs.

We have already established the premise that most people want to be successful and do a good job, so why has she chosen not to perform? To unravel the reason a particular employee is *insubordinate,* it is important to realize that at this point in the investigation, or the peeling back of the onion, we are assuming that it is the CHOICE of the person not to complete the task. There are no other barriers with equipment or her capabilities that are preventing her progress. For whatever reason...she has chosen not to complete the task and now the problem remains to figure out why.

Now you are truly at the "last man standing" rule. If you have given the employee everything available systemically, and matched him with a job commensurate with his talents and skills, and he still does not perform, the person is the problem. This person can be described as self-sabotaging, lazy, passive-aggressive, or slow-rolling. He enjoys undermining leadership and/or the organization. This worker is negative and a pot-stirrer who thrives on chaos. He displays a dysfunctional personality. He is now officially and accurately categorized as *insubordinate*!

It should now be clear that this is a leadership issue and it is a discipline problem. It is not a training problem. You have to hold that person accountable with clear guidelines, established milestones and a mandatory performance

If they could have, they already would have

improvement plan (PIP)...and then, if he does not perform, the only thing left to do is to fire him.

That is important. If you do not fire people for unwillingness to do their jobs, you are doing a disservice to those 98 percent who are wonderful employees who are willingly and capably doing their jobs. (Moreover, they know who is not pulling his weight.) When you fire under-performing employees, you have said loud and clear, "We're only going to carry people with the highest standards." If you let this *insubordinate* person, who is very capable, and very smart, and has all the resources, slide by in spite of the fact that he is lazy and lacking a good work ethic, you will de-motivate the other great people. This is wrong. It is wrong on many levels, but one level to consider is that you are not doing that person any favors either. You are telling him that his behaviors are okay. You are training him to keep doing what he has been doing. You have enabled him to continue making dysfunctional decisions.

I have been fired three times. I am obviously very hard-headed and did not get the message the first two times. I deserved to be fired. I *deserved* it. Repeat: *I deserved it.* Those supervisors who fired me did me a favor by making sure I understood that I was smart and capable, but I was *insubordinate* and unwilling to be productive in the organization. It is very important to acknowledge that sometimes the right answer is to fire people! I returned to thank each of them later for firing me.

If they could have, they already would have

Do not try to be a charity-jobs-program. Do not "rescue" insubordinate employees. You will never get to an "outstanding attracts outstanding" level in your organization that way. It is not the right answer. You are not sending the people the right signal. You are training them that it is okay to be slugs. You are saying it is okay to be a negative influence within your organization. As a leader, you will be spending 80 percent of your time dealing with this 20 percent of the people, mitigating the same issues repeatedly. No matter where you move them around within the organization, they will exhibit and execute their behaviors the same way again-and-again. You will be spreading the problem around among all your supervisors. You will spend innumerable hours trying to keep your organization functioning around them. Your star performers *will leave because they can.* They get so fed up picking up the slack for the sub-performers. Good people can always find another job because other organizations are always looking for good people.

You need to pull off that Band-Aid quickly and cleanly. You need to put in place 30, 60, and 90-day improvement plans, and if he does not turn around, let him go. You need to do it sooner rather than later. Do not let things linger. It does not matter what the offense is, whether it is laziness, insubordination, or egregious sexual harassment; whatever it is, accountability has to be swift.

Unfortunately, leaders do not always do a good job with enforcing accountability. If a person becomes a problem, we tend to shuffle them into other departments, called the "Office of Special Projects," where the dysfunction

If they could have, they already would have

becomes someone else's concern. We take the easy way out instead of doing the hard work of documenting problem behavior and dealing with the person head on.

Everyone needs to know that "outstanding attracts outstanding." There is no room for less than the highest possible standards within your organization. That is what it is going to take to survive in this global marketplace. You have to hang on to your edge, because everyone else is catching up. Your competitors have these answers too.

If they could have, they already would have

Chapter 3

First Line Supervisors

The single most powerful influence in an organization is the *first line supervisor*. This leader holds the heartbeat of the organization in his hands. As a manager, you set the beat for the first line supervisors. When dealing with employees, the first line supervisor needs to "train 'em, trust 'em, get out of the way, and be there to pick up the pieces or pat 'em on the back."

Train them!

Train them on all the rules and regulations they have to live by. Train them to the highest competency standards, not just babysitting the status quo (i.e. the way we have always done it!). Train them to make decisions the way you would.

Trust them!

Train them well, and then you can trust them. People are amazing. They can be ingenious when getting the job done. The young workers of today never cease to amaze me. They are so computer and electronic-savvy. They can do things that I have not even imagined. Give them direction and resources, then…get out of the way!

If they could have, they already would have

Get out of their way!

This is the empowerment step. Empower people with tools, resources, training, boundaries, clear guidance, explicit objectives, and opportunities. They will do amazing things.

Be there to pick up the pieces!

This is the feedback step. We are only human; sometimes we step outside the boundaries and need a course correction. Give them specific and timely feedback and bring them back on course. If they are willing, able and capable, this is a normal part of the job.

Pat them on the back!

This is the recognition step. I am sure you have heard the cliché, "We have done so much for so long with so little; we can do anything with nothing." We ask so much of our people; they deserve to be recognized with promotions, rewards, or a simple, "Thank you!"

As a first line supervisor for a large manufacturing plant, I taught technical classes for the employees. Every class they completed resulted in a ten-cent raise. The classes were offered outside their normal shifts and on weekends. I had a Saturday morning class to teach before I headed out on a week's vacation. I went to work dressed casually in jeans and a t-shirt. This was not my normal attire and very casual for me. One student asked me, "So what's going on; why are you dressed so casually?" I answered, "I'm on vacation, and I am leaving right after this class." He paused, looked at me solemnly, and said quietly, "You make me feel important." This forklift driver had worked there for over twenty years and, in his mind, no one in

If they could have, they already would have

management had ever sacrificed anything for him. Here was a chance for him to make ten cents an hour more, and I gave him that. To me, it was a responsibility and a commitment I had made to the employees. I would provide the classes if they would attend on their own time so they would learn and grow. I held up my end of the bargain. In the end, I was the one blessed with this wonderful man, this very gracious gentleman, who was grateful to have a job, grateful to get a ten-cent raise, and tell me these magical words, "You make me feel important."

I do not think a first line supervisor can do anything more important than to let every person know his worth, his value, and his importance in the bigger picture. If you put him on the line--a production line, a manufacturing line, or in an office--and say, "Put A before B, and B before C and C before D, that is all you need to do," it is a terrible disservice. If you do not ever tell each worker why he is doing what he is doing, or how he fits into the bigger picture, then how can you ever develop his loyalty to the organization, loyalty to the company, pride in doing a good job, or pride in being the best employee he can possibly be?

If we want "outstanding to attract outstanding," we have to make our workers feel important and make them feel as if they, too, are winning when the overall organization wins. I think that is why compensation needs to be tied to performance and not paid as a bonus, but tied to the return on investment of the organization itself.

First line supervisors are the key to building this loyalty; but in many cases, they are new to the role of supervisor and not trained on how to proceed, especially if they have

If they could have, they already would have

come up through the ranks and are now supervising their friends.

All supervisors or managers, regardless of where they sit, have to provide employees with *PRIDE & SPIRIT* to be able to *REAP* the benefits of *LUCK*.

- *PRIDE* - *P*ower, *R*esponsibility, *I*dentity, *D*irection, *E*nergy
- *SPIRIT* - *S*upport, *P*roblem-solving, *I*mportance, *R*ecognition, *I*nterest, *T*rust
- *REAP* - *R*esources, *E*vidence, *A*uthority, *P*raise
- *LUCK* - *L*istened to, *U*nderstood, *C*ommunication, *K*nowledge

If any of these items are missing, then the opposite will occur. They will be *FINISHED*:

- *FINISHED*
    - *F*eelings of not being heard; disengaged
    - *I*nadequate time for problem solving; reactionary
    - *N*ot enough resources; unable
    - *I*ndecisive and confused about organizational objectives
    - *S*hort-changed out of success, growth and development
    - *H*ostile to leaders and the organization
    - *E*mbarrassed by being treated as an interchangeable part
    - *D*evastated by the lack of trust

The flow of *PRIDE*, *SPIRIT*, and the ability to *REAP* the benefits of *LUCK* in the workforce cannot happen just once during employees' initial orientation week; it has to be refined and reinforced daily by all levels of management, but most importantly, it must emanate from the first line supervisor.

Feedback

The most powerful tool in the first line supervisor's toolbox is the ability to give *feedback*.

Feedback is more than just a word. It is critical in growing new leaders. Feedback needs to be delivered consistently. The timing for feedback with new employees should be monthly at a minimum, and given during on-the-spot corrections. For employees who have been with the organization for two-to-three years, formal feedback should happen on a quarterly basis in addition to timely on-the-spot corrections. For more seasoned employees with four-to-five years, the feedback should occur semi-annually and during on-the-spot corrections. After five-plus years, the employees should move! Your feedback sessions over the years should have been grooming them for their next assignment, job, or promotion.

Effective feedback sessions with employees allow them to maintain their self-esteem. It is imperative that you listen and respond with empathy. It helps to get them involved in the organization by asking for help to solve problems. By just saying, "I need your help…" opens new doors for them. When it comes to their work, you need to offer help without taking responsibility from them. Your role is that of a mentor. This is where the lines of delegation must be clear. Many great feedback methods are available to be used to implement a formal system. The effective techniques allow the workers to provide input and set their

If they could have, they already would have

own goals. As long as the system is implemented consistently, the specific method is not that important.

Different however, is the day-to-day or on-the-spot feedback. On-the-spot feedback is critical in relaying your commitment to never to walk past a mistake. This campaign is covered in a later chapter, but the baseline rule is that if you walk by a mistake or a problem, you are sending the message that you condone that behavior. On-the-spot feedback will set that record straight.

You can provide positive or negative feedback by using the BASICs Feedback technique:

B	BEHAVIOR	What was the behavior you observed? Describe the exact behaviors (good or bad) as displayed by the employee. Do not editorialize or give opinions; reflect back exactly what you observed.
A	ATTITUDE	What was the attitude you observed? Describe the attitude displayed by the employee during the inappropriate behaviors. If he did something good, then describe his great attitude. If he did something negative, then describe the attitude he exhibited during that behavior. If applicable, describe how his behaviors affected the attitudes of the people around him.

If they could have, they already would have

S	STANDARD	What standard was exemplified or violated (Regulations, Standard Operating Procedures, Technical Orders, Office Work policies, Employee Handbook rule, etc.)? Identify the exact organizational rule or procedure that was violated; quote the specific paragraph, if possible.
I	IMPACT	What was the impact of the behavior? Describe the positive or negative impact his behaviors and attitudes had on himself, his peers, and his subordinates. Describe how he did or did not set the example for others. Describe how his behavior affected the mission.
C	CONSE-QUENCES	What are the consequences of the behavior? Delineate the consequences of the actions. If he did something good, let him know there are positive consequences: promotions, program management opportunities, increased roles and responsibilities, and senior leader recognition. If the behaviors were negative, define clearly what the negative consequences are now and will be if the negative behavior and attitude are continued.

If they could have, they already would have

| S | SOLUTIONS | What is the solution to eliminate this behavior or situation? If the behavior was negative, define a course of action that the employee will take to improve. Get the employee to agree to the solutions. Ask the employee first, "What are you going to do to fix this behavior and/or attitude?" Then write down his solution and add your own expectations, with specific timelines. |

Create a template BASICS form; use it to document the conversation. If the feedback happens in passing or on-the-spot (for positive or negative reasons), document the conversation on one of your BASICS forms when you get back to your desk. This documentation is used later for rewards and recognition as well as consequences.

Rules of Engagement (ROEs):

➢ Ensure you have a witness for all negative feedback. If possible, ensure you have a witness representing the same demographics as the employee receiving feedback (gender, race, national origin, etc.)

➢ Remove any hint of discrimination during a negative feedback session. The best way to ensure there is no perceived discrimination is to reflect back to the employee his own behaviors. Do not include your own opinions! State the facts only.

If they could have, they already would have

> ➢ Ask the employee to sign a Memorandum for Record (MFR). If the employee refuses to sign, write in the statement, "Employee refused to sign." Then have the witness sign under this statement. Even if the employee does not sign the MFR, have the witness sign it.

Providing timely feedback enables the person to see firsthand to what you are referring. If you wait until later-- a day, a week or until his next formal feedback session-- the lesson will be lost. Here is an example. I was walking through my office area and heard a young man telling an unprofessional joke to his co-workers. There were several people present, both males and females. I could tell by their half-hearted laughter that the joke was not well received and several people just wished the guy would shut up. As I passed the group, I asked the comedian if I could talk to him when he had a chance. It was important for me not to embarrass him in front of his peers.

When the employee stopped by my office a few minutes later, I asked him if I could provide him with some feedback. I was not his supervisor, nor in his direct chain of command, so I felt the need to ask instead of just unloading on him. I prefer to ask permission from anyone to whom I want to provide feedback when they are not my direct subordinates. I have found that it is a very rare occasion when someone will say, "No, I don't want to hear what you have to say." It also starts the conversation as a partnership, not a one-way blasting.

After this young man sat down, I ran through the BASICS feedback outline with him:

If they could have, they already would have

B	BEHAVIOR	You were telling what may have been seen as an inappropriate joke in the workplace.
A	ATTITUDE	When you were telling your joke you were focused on the punch line, so I do not believe that you were aware of how it was being received by the others. Some of the people did not appreciate your humor and appeared to be offended.
S	STANDARD	In a work environment or in any professional situation, you need to think twice before you speak. As a rule of thumb, ask yourself, "Is this something I would say in front of my mother or my grandmother?" It is important to realize that people have varying tolerance levels for humor and can easily be offended, which results in them feeling uncomfortable in their work area.
I	IMPACT	Your co-workers may not receive you so warmly in the future and they might tend to shy away from you or want to dis-associate from you as they do not want to be associated with that type of behavior. This type of environment does not lend itself to a healthy, happy workplace.
C	CONSE-QUENCES	At the extreme end of the spectrum, if someone was truly offended by your joke, he would have a valid case to file a grievance against you. At the very

If they could have, they already would have

		least, you have made the work place uncomfortable and you may find that others treat you differently in the future. I want you to realize that this is our private conversation, and I am not planning to take further action on this matter. I will bring it to your supervisor's attention if I hear of it occurring a second time, however. I will keep a copy of this BASICS memo in my drawer and will only pull it out if I have to write a second one. Then I will bring both memos to your supervisor as documentation that you have been warned.
S	SOLUTIONS	I am not planning to take further action on this matter at this time; however, you may chose to do so. It probably would pay you dividends if you went back into that same circle of co-workers and apologized for your insensitivity. I think you would set the record straight with them and also earn their respect and trust. I ask you to think about what I have said, and I thank you for listening to my feedback.

The young man did go back and talk to his co-workers. It actually led them to create an office rule of engagement about the types of jokes that were acceptable and not acceptable among them as a work team. You still heard

63

If they could have, they already would have

laughter in their section; but it was not based on unprofessional and inappropriate scenarios.

The goal of feedback is to change behavior or attitudes. When it works, everyone wins. The employee is more successful and does not repeat mistakes. The first line supervisor spends less time on corrective actions, and organizational productivity increases in efficiency and effectiveness.

Some people will not respond well to feedback. That leads to a different conversation. The next discussion will be about whether the employee's inability to receive professional feedback is an indication of bigger issues. Perhaps the employee is not a good fit for the organization at all.

The use of the BASICs Feedback template is intended to minimize confrontation and focus on quick fixes to problems or deviations from organizational standards. This tool can be used verbally or in writing. Handwritten copies of the documentation are as effective as typed copies. The words are important, not the form.

Delegation

Another key to effective first line leadership is *delegation*. It is learning when to hold 'em and when to pass 'em on. Delegating is difficult. You know that you could do the job yourself better or faster and may not want to take the time or effort to teach someone else how to do the job or educate others on the requirements. The bottom line is that you cannot do it all yourself. Even if you could, you are limiting the growth potential of your employees. So you need to learn how to delegate effectively.

When you delegate, you must first ensure that you refer the task to the right person. Next, you must decide to delegate the authority to carry out the task and to make decisions, or to delegate the task without giving decision-making authority. It will depend on the worker's maturity, skills and knowledge at the time. Whatever the outcome of the authority level, you must allow the worker to keep the task and work it. It is important that you set up controls for course corrections along the way, if needed. A boss who over-controls or one who abandons control sets his people up for failure. Success comes from the boss who uses situational control with his people. People respond negatively to controls when they are inappropriate for the situation. It is important to remember, however, that sharing responsibility does not mean abandoning responsibility.

The leader still has the responsibility to know what is going on, set the direction for the department, make the decisions her employees cannot, ensure that people are on course, offer a guiding hand, open doors to clear the way, assess performance, and be a smart manager of resources.

If they could have, they already would have

To get the job done, you have to channel the action in the right direction by mutually establishing the following:

- Key Result Areas (the direction we want to go)
- Measurements (to know we are going in right direction)
- Goals (Are we there yet? How would you know?)
- Feedback (constant and compared to goals)
  - let people manage their own feedback system in setting goals, and
  - change measures and goals to motivate people in new directions.

Coaching

Coaching is a primary duty of a supervisor. Coaching makes a new project exciting and challenging! In one situation, I was tasked to roll out a major project that we all knew would not be well received and required a lot of work from the people on top of their other duties. I broke the task requirements down into three teams: Red, Yellow, and Green. After the long meeting of explaining the project and the tasks involved, I announced the appointment of people to each of the teams. I then unveiled a tier of cupcakes frosted in red, yellow or green. Everyone was invited to get a cupcake that represented his appointment. The meeting ended with everyone smiling, mingling with their new team members, and enjoying their treats. Not a bad way to start down a tough road!

People learn faster from successes than they do from failures. A way to ensure success is to have a process to follow. A systematic approach to coaching results in the following steps:

1. Explain the purpose and importance of what you are teaching.
2. Explain the process to be used.
3. Show or demonstrate how it is done.
4. Observe while the person practices the process.
5. Provide immediate and specific feedback (coach, reinforce success).
6. Express confidence in the person's ability to be successful.
7. Agree on follow-on actions.

It is important to follow through once the initial training or orientation is complete. You need to use key principles to overcome blockage and slippage. The key principles are to ensure self-esteem, listen with empathy, and offer help without taking responsibility. It is also vital that you compare the current performance level against the improved performance goals, and share the gains publicly.

Key Principles

Anytime you establish a group to work together as a team there will be growing pains. An effective team can really energize performance. On the other hand, a team riddled with ego problems and power struggles can be self-defeating. A point to remember with effective teams is that the more decisions a team can make on its own, the more energized and empowered the employees will be. When you run into blockages such as defensiveness, anger, or

If they could have, they already would have

mistrust, you must employ *key principles* to deal with these as well.

I had the pleasure of teaching a Team Building course at a mining organization. The teams had been organized by the company leadership prior to my arrival. The first exercise was to ensure that we had the right employees on each team. One team realized it was missing a vital employee crucial to the overall process. I went to the company leaders and told them we needed a specific employee to represent a particular step in the process. They huddled together, called that section, and an employee was there by the next break.

During that break, one of the front-line workers walked up to me and said, "Who are you? Why do they listen to you?" He was frankly amazed at how quickly the team's wishes were executed. I told him that the company leaders trusted me (and were paying me) to give them the right answers. I knew that the right answers were found inside the team. By the way, that team saved the company millions of dollars in the next few years. They were so empowered by that immediate response from the leadership that they were dedicated to getting incredible results from that moment on.

To have effective teams the members need to have a clear understanding of what is expected of their team. This is a crucial second step (after you ensure you have all the right employees) to ensure that their charter is clear and that all the team employees know where they are headed.

If they could have, they already would have

You need to:

- Establish the mission or charter for the team.
- Provide a time and place for the team to meet.
- Provide technical training at the teachable moments.
- Provide communication skills for interacting, solving problems, making decisions, and taking action.

A well-oiled team can take lots of responsibility and will amaze you with its outcomes. If provided a stable foundation and allowed to perform, team employees generally will.

They should be capable of:

- Determining who works on what.
- Handling internal absenteeism and performance issues.
- Getting involved in all aspects of their work.
- Selecting their own team leader based on their tasks.
- Finding opportunities to improve quality and productivity (and work to realize those opportunities.)
- Performing basic maintenance.
- Scheduling vacations and time off while still meeting deadlines!

At some point in the process, you have to ask yourself, "Who is responsible for a team's or employee's success or

If they could have, they already would have

failure?" and "Who determines how engaged or disengaged an employee is?" Your first response is to believe that the person himself is ultimately responsible for his success. However, there are other factors that must be reviewed to ensure that all roadblocks are removed. The list of areas to evaluate are as follows:

1. The person's IMMEDIATE boss (the first line supervisor.)
2. The other people who affect the person's job.
3. Higher management.
4. The organization and its systems.

By far the most important influence to an employee is the supervisor to whom the employee directly reports! It is crucial to ensure that you are enabling your employees and not inadvertently disabling their efforts. It is important to remember that nothing is a secret on the front line. People will make things up if the data they are given is poor. (We all have to deal with the "grapevine reality." About 95 percent of the information is accurate; however that last five percent is a doozy and may take you way off course.)

Management's role in ensuring there is an enabling environment is to constantly review the current radar screen, scan the horizon for upcoming concerns and stay one step ahead of the work train. You will need to:

1. Protect people from the disabling things that the company might attempt to put upon them while supporting and encouraging the enabling aspects the company can offer.

If they could have, they already would have

2. Be sure that subordinate managers have the skills required to enable their personnel. If not, get them trained.
3. Model the enabled, high-performing behavior.
4. Coach subordinate managers in how to use and improve their enabling skills.
5. Reward performance resulting from enabled employees.

You need to create an environment where wonderful things can happen. In an environment of enabled employees, and with increases in productivity, you are going to have a number of talented people in the organization with less and less to do. Think about putting together one of these talented teams to develop new businesses into which you can shift underutilized people and which can generate more income for the company. It is essential to keep the momentum going. Once the train is rolling down the track, keep learning, keep improving, and keep growing. Do not stop and do not give up.

At one location there was a team that kept derailing without ever producing. I was asked to facilitate for this team to see if I could get them back on track. My task was to take a hard look at the makeup of the team and to find out from where the problems stemmed. What I found out really startled me, but also made me realize what an isolated world my paradigms covered. This was a team of manufacturing line workers brought together to see about improving the line process. The following illustrates how important it is for the supervisor to listen and observe.

If they could have, they already would have

All the employees of this team were younger African American males, or so I thought. But after peeling back the onion in a few meetings I found out that the problem revolved around discrimination among the employees themselves. It so happened that they were not all African Americans in their own eyes. There were African American blacks that were born in America, then there were African American blacks that were born in Africa and immigrated to the United States, and then there were Jamaican blacks that were either born in Jamaica or still had strong affiliations with Jamaica, and there were Brazilian blacks. This group measured each other's worth based on where they were born or with which country they affiliated.

The person who was assigned as the team leader was from Brazil, and was considered to be at the bottom of this social totem pole. And that was just one of their issues. I was flabbergasted to find out the degree of prejudice that he was dealing with. No wonder they were having problems functioning as a team…they were having problems functioning as equal human beings.

This team had a lot of learning, growing, and understanding to accomplish before they could function cohesively. It took a lot of hard work and soul-searching on everyone's part. It is important to ensure your teams are as cohesive as possible, and if not, provide the appropriate team or awareness training necessary.

If they could have, they already would have

GRACE

We all have experienced a time when we were faced with dealing with a new boss or co-worker and knew that it took time to learn the ropes about how to interact with that person. What were his perspectives, what was their frame of reference? This honeymoon period was fraught with the need to impress the new boss, build trust, and demonstrate your skills. Frequently, though, the bumps in the road came down to miscommunication and varying expectations. You could easily walk away thinking you were on the same page as that person only to find out later--after the deadline for the project had passed—that you were hearing "apples" when he was saying "oranges," or at least hearing "oranges" when he was saying "tangerines." This likely led to lost productivity and even more important, frustration. For example, have you ever heard yourself or others say something like, "I could have done it that way if only I had known that was what you wanted. I assumed you were only looking for the data from this year; I did not know you were interested in past years' performance." The list of miscommunication can go on and on. At this point, you may be thinking, "We never seem to have time to do it right the first time, but we always seem to have time to do it over." When this happens, I think to myself, "Lord, give me *grace*."

Every leadership class, book or process I have ever experienced talked about techniques for clarifying expectations, listening, or negotiating to agreement. Employees will darn near kill themselves trying to accomplish the mission, and that is why clear

If they could have, they already would have

understanding is so critical. One of the most frustrating things I have encountered as an employee is to get an assignment, go off and bust my butt accomplishing that task, only to hear my supervisors say, "Wow, that looks great but it is not exactly what I was looking for. Could you change it to this or add that?"

Of course I could change it, and did so willingly, but the frustration lay in having to do the rework. I could have easily done it the other way in the first place, if they had only asked or I had clearly understood what they wanted. I do not think supervisors do this intentionally, but it happens all the time in both very small and large ways.

I needed *grace* to get through these kinds of days…my own outline for what I needed from my boss to effectively do my job or what I need to share with my subordinates or co-workers so they could also do their jobs right the first time. *GRACE* stands for Goals, Resources, Abilities, Consequences and Evaluation. If I covered each one of these categories prior to beginning a project, then I could feel reasonably sure that all involved had the same end in mind, and guess what--it worked. Running this process is not something that needs to be formally apparent in all situations. You run the categories in your head and keep getting clarification from the boss until you have what you need. My co-workers and subordinates are now used to my *GRACE* and normally guide their discussions down that path.

If they could have, they already would have

GRACE WORKSHEET

G	Goals	Directions, guidelines, deliverables, milestones	What is the end in mind or what is the purpose/audience for the project? What are the rules or guidelines I need to play by or boundaries to stay within?
R	Resources	Tools, time, money, people, policies	What resources do I have to work with? It is helpful to run through the five M's to ensure that all bases are covered. Money--how much can I spend? Manpower--do I have anyone who can help me? Materials--are there any supplies or materials in support of this project? Method--is there a specific layout or process that I should use? Machines--do I have access to needed technology?
A	Abilities	Skill levels, check back points	Do I need prior approval on any of it, and if so whom do I see? Does the supervisor want me to check back with him at each stage?
C	Consequences	Boundaries, outcomes, rewards	Who is to be involved, or who I can share the data with at this time? What happens if it does not get done? What happens if it does get done? What/when and to whom am I accountable to on this project? Does the supervisor want to see the project at milestones along the way or just a finished product? What kind of deadline is there? What happens if I am unable to

If they could have, they already would have

			complete or meet the deadline? What happens if I meet or exceed the deadline? Whom will it affect? Are there financial consequences (positive or negative) associated with it?
E	Evaluation	Feedback	How will I know how well I did? What areas were lacking, or what areas were over-engineered? How can it be handled better in the future? What was the level of satisfaction from all parties involved—team, customers, or stockholders?

Using the *GRACE* checklist has simplified and clarified my life more than I could have ever dreamed. These clarifying questions allowed me to do the job right the first time. I am not saying that some projects did not need revision or changes, but they did not occur because of a misunderstanding of the task at hand. Living with *GRACE* works not only at work, but at home and in every other aspect of my life because it is a tool for clarification and understanding. That is something we need anytime we have a conversation with another human being. I would like to share an example from the home front.

Let us say your 13-year old teenager wants to go the movies, with her friends, by herself without interference. After all, she is all grown up now--right? Or at least *she* thinks so. This is a wonderful time to deploy GRACE.

If they could have, they already would have

G	Goals	You want to have fun with your friends and I want you to be safe and behave in a manner that meets our family's standards. So here are the movies you can choose from. None that are rated R. You are not allowed, nor are you legally of age, to attend an R-rated movie. Here are the times you can pick from. Here are the theaters you can go to. You must tell me in advance whom you are planning on meeting there, and I want to see the clothes you plan to wear in advance.
R	Resources	I will pay for the movie ticket and you pay for any snacks or drinks. I will take you to the theater and I will pick you up. Yes, I will drop you off a safe distance from the door if you like, so that your friends will not see how you got there.
A	Abilities	As this is new level of freedom for you, I want to make sure you are choosing wisely. You must keep your cell phone with you and you must call me if anything changes with your plans. I mean call, as in talking…no texting. I want to be able to speak to you to discuss what is going on. You will remain outfitted as you were when you left the house. No extra makeup, no different clothes, no extra bling.
C	Conse-quences	I will be outside the theater at our designated spot 30 minutes after the movie ends. This should give you sufficient time to powder your nose, discuss the movie and say goodbye to your friends. If you are not out at the car as we discussed and I have not received a phone call explaining why, then I will come in looking for you. I will find you and it may be embarrassing.
E	Evaluation	You are going out on a Saturday night, but that does not change the fact that you need to be up on Sunday morning ready to go, as we have plans for that day. If you do not get up on the first call on Sunday morning, I can only conclude that you cannot handle doing two diverse things on a weekend. That will be the first evaluation point. Then I would like you to tell me how the movie was and how you felt the night went. If we both did our parts then it builds trust between us. This can be a pre-test for the dance you want to go to next month.

All in all, the event went well for both parties and both of our expectations were met. We used *GRACE* consistently to negotiate teen adventures.

If they could have, they already would have

GRACE WORKSHEET

Notes

Goals

Regulations	Manuals
Operating Instructions	
Laws	Business Plans
Policies	Timelines
Templates	Benchmarks
Spec Sheets	

Resources

Manpower	Money
Machine	Methods
Mentors	
SMEs	

Abilities

Levels of Empowerment	Feedback
Feedback	Milestones
Meet-ups	Periodic Checks
Resources needed	

If they could have, they already would have

Consequences	Intended	Made submission	
	Team effort	Superior performers	
	Rewards	Professional	
	Unintended	Lost ops	
	Lowered morale	Not in compliance	
	Not worthy of trust	No bonus	
Evaluation	Feedback	Mid-course corrections	
	Cycle evaluations	Cont. Improvement	
	Formal/Informal		
	Metrics		

If they could have, they already would have

Habits

"We are what we repeatedly do. Excellence, then, is not an act, but a habit."

Aristotle

There is much talk and theorizing on what makes a leader. Some say leaders are born, other say they are created by their environment. I feel it is probably a combination of both. It does appear that certain types of personalities lend themselves to becoming great leaders, but all in all, leaders are people who have good habits when dealing with and motivating people. Habits are not something we inherit at birth; they are learned by repetition of action. To create a new habit or skill you need to do the following:

1. Gain the knowledge--what to do and why.
2. Develop the skill--how to do it.
3. Flame the desire—want to do it.

Science tells us that it takes repeating an action at least twenty-one times for our brains to develop it into a new habit. What this tells me is that I will have to give out twenty-one feedback template letters before it becomes a habit for me to reach for one every time I give feedback-- good and bad.

Ineptitude

One of the hardest challenges that a supervisor must deal with is ineptitude. The dictionary describes it as "the quality or state of being inept; *incompetent, unfit, etc.*

If they could have, they already would have

In our world, ineptitude is shrouded in red herrings and diversions and ends up costing leadership and management hours and hours of time to fight.

An inept employee operates from the position of fear: fear of discovery (of the ineptitude), and fear of loss of job or identity ("If I have a job, I have value.") The inept person fights with the tools the system created for him or her. He will use Inspector General complaints, union grievances, Human Resources office actions claiming a hostile work environment, Equal Employment Opportunity complaints, or whistleblower protections, all the while rationalizing, "I am not the problem."

Granted, some complaints are valid, and these systems are intended for use in legitimate scenarios. It is when the inept employee feels cornered or powerless that he turns to the company's systemic structure as a last resort to ward off accountability.

The inept employee blames others for her problems with claims of undue stress, hostility, being untrained, or not given reasonable expectations. The only protection or defense for the leader or manager is documentation, documentation and more documentation. You need to have a detailed timeline and spreadsheet of every action taken by you and the employee. It must include every step and include the whole-person concept to highlight trends. For example, a trend might be regular use of sick or annual leave coinciding with work deadlines or physical training requirements. Another example might be delaying physical training testing because of a newly diagnosed medical issue. The worker might also claim that mental health

If they could have, they already would have

stressors caused by the environment as the reason for a lack of productivity.

The only way to battle this enemy of productivity is through diligent, dedicated performance documentation and feedback. It must be broken down into the smallest bite-sized elements that are irrefutable and understandable to all. You need to share the plan with all employees of the same office. As an example, you might have to make all the workers in an office keep daily logs of their productivity. The results will show vividly if one employee differs in his production rates.

In one office, I had an employee who I knew was not pulling her weight, but in the past nothing had been documented. I had inherited ineptitude. We had all four of the workers in that section keep daily logs of their workload. The logs proved she did five entries per day versus the others' 20 per day. In the end, I was able to prove her dereliction of duty. Two weeks after she was gone, the others came to me to say that her absence created zero increase in any of their individual workload, and that they were shocked because they had not realized how little productivity she provided to the organization. They realized they had already been carrying her load.

Mentoring

I was being especially tough on one of my employees because I knew she was capable of so much more than she was producing. I had threatened to fire her two years earlier. I said, "You are not living up to your potential; you have a lousy attitude. You are awkward to work with and

If they could have, they already would have

no one wants to work with you. This is not right. You need to do more, and to be a better co-worker."

I really pushed her hard and even transferred her to one of the toughest organizations in our Wing. I knew it was going to be tough on her. The new position dealt mostly with personnel issues.

After two weeks she came back crying her eyes out. "They'll never respect me; they ignore me, they laugh at me, they undermine me." Blah, blah, blah. I said, "Stop it! You are better than this. You have a bachelor's degree; most of them do not even have a two-year degree. You get back over there and you earn their trust. Here's how you do it. You find something you can do to make their jobs easier. Find something you can do to make their lives easier. Take a burden off their shoulders."

It took a long time for her to earn trust and credibility and for the senior NCOs to begin to turn to her as a resource. It was a long while before they began to come and ask for her advice or for assistance, or to see her as a trusted ally. But she did it.

Previously, she had gone into a leadership course and after two weeks, once again, she said, "It is too hard. It is too hard to work full time and go to school at night; there is a lot of homework. There is just so much to do. Can I quit?"

I said, "No! You are not going to quit! That is nonsense. You have a bachelor's degree; this is a school setting. Just because you went to school full time for your bachelor's degree does not mean you cannot learn how to work and go to school at night now." In the end, she loved the

If they could have, they already would have

experience so much, she volunteered and went through the training to become one of the instructors for future classes.

It was tough love, applied strategically, to allow the employee to know, "You have potential! You are not living up to that potential and I am not going to let you take the easy way out." On both counts, she succeeded. What she did not do, though, was knock out another required leadership academy course in time to apply for a wonderful job opportunity. And she was crushed.

I said to her, "You need to tell your story to the others during our next staff meeting and let them know what you learned. You have to take care of your own career too. You were so busy taking care of everyone else, you did not take care of yourself."

She not only told the story about her professional military education dilemma, she also took the time to tell others, "I haven't always understood my boss' mentoring moments when she was tough on me, but she forced me to grow. She forced me to learn about myself, to stretch, and I am now a different person; a better person because of it."

I was lucky to be able to hear about the impact I had on an employee's life. Most of the time you are not going to get direct feedback, but what you need to know is: it is happening whether they tell you or not! If you are a first line supervisor, you are the single most important and influential person in any organization...military, government, service, computers, technology, or manufacturing--no matter what the industry.

If they could have, they already would have

You are the single most impactful person in the life of your employees and you have to know that people are watching you 24/7. If you do not follow the rules, why should they? You can never get away with, "Do as I say, not as I do!" It is never going to work. You have to be on your A-game at all times. You have to hold people accountable and you have to keep your own standards high.

If you lower your standards, you tell everyone in your organization, "I'm not capable of anything better, not capable of anything more, so why should I expect you to do anything more?" If you lower the standards to the lowest common denominator, then that is all you are going to get.

Attitude

We choose our *attitude* in every situation, whether we know it or not. Our attitude determines our approach to life and leadership style.

There is a fine line between "confident" and "cocky." Humble confidence will be appreciated by your senior leaders, peers and subordinates. Cocky is not an attitude that is generally well-received.

Cocky is thinking that you are better than everyone else, that you are a genius and God's gift to your company. Just because you think you are a genius, does not mean that you are going to be successful. If you are cocky, you are going to irritate people. They are not going to want to work with you, and in the final analysis, work gets done through relationships. Work does not get done through

If they could have, they already would have

organizations. You should not say, "I'm going to call Human Resources." No, there are people behind the job titles. You are going to call Mrs. Smith who works in Human Resources. You are going to call Bobbi; you are going to call Stephanie. You are not going to call an ephemeral organization; you are going to call a person, because there is no other entity who can answer the phone until we get that artificial intelligence thing working better. Work gets done through relationships. You have to establish those relationships so that when you need help, you will know who you can count on or who to ask.

You cannot lead with your arrogance, because people are going to shut you down. They are probably going to be passive-aggressive about it and will not challenge you because most people will behave in a professional manner. Most people are going to want to avoid conflict, but in the end, you are going to lose because your attitude violates basic principles. Principles are guidelines for human conduct that are proven to have enduring, permanent value.

These are the guidelines that we must strive to live by:

- Fairness (even little children know this one without being taught)
- Integrity
- Honesty
- Trust
- Cooperation
- Personal and interpersonal growth
- Human dignity
- Service

If they could have, they already would have

- ➢ Quality
- ➢ Excellence
- ➢ Nurturance
- ➢ Encouragement

If you do not believe this, try living with the opposite principles. How is that going to work out? Will you be successful? Take a look:

- ➢ Unfairness
- ➢ Deceit
- ➢ Baseness
- ➢ Uselessness
- ➢ Mediocrity
- ➢ Degeneration

Do any of those qualities sound exciting to work with?

When dealing with others your attitude is important. Your attitude determines your altitude: how high you can go. Only basic underlying goodness gives life to the technique. The successful use of the techniques of open communication or "cheering on the troops to the next level of achievement" are dependent upon your attitude. In whatever challenge you undertake, your attitude is key. If your attitude is demeaning or you are perceived as manipulative, your success will only exist when your back is not turned.

Our attitude determines our relationships with people. People have to buy into *you* before they will buy into your leadership. The key to how you treat people is how you think about them. You have to believe in your people. It is

If they could have, they already would have

easier to dismiss someone than it is to train them, but dismissal is not the answer. You have to help him to succeed. Most people are genuinely grateful when you make them feel important. When you help one person, you are impacting a lot of other people as well. The word will spread. Each one will teach one.

Often our attitude is the major difference between success and failure. I read an interesting statistic about Olympic competitors: An analysis of the difference between Olympic gold medal and silver medal winners revealed the average time difference (in all timed events) was only one-tenth of a second. It is hard to believe one athlete is physically better for one-tenth of a second compared to his opponent. The difference has to be mental attitude: that confidence, that ability to overcome setbacks, deal with discouragement, and put out 110 percent and not let up in the face of adversity.

That 110 percent must be the application of continuous improvement and a willingness to stretch—making the effort to go beyond your comfort zone to reach new levels. We have to keep moving our targets further out to ensure that we keep growing.

Leaders believe in people. Most people do not believe in themselves and rarely does a person succeed when he does not believe. Most people can tell when someone believes in themselves. You have to *act* positively, not just *think* positively. Be the leader you want to become. Choose to have a positive attitude in dealing with setbacks, discouragement, or stress. You will improve your well-being and you will role model the attitude and behavior that you want your followers to have. Most people will do everything they can to reinforce a leader's belief in them.

Leaders connect with people. People do not care how much you know, until they know how much you care! Praise people and show honest appreciation. Call attention to mistakes indirectly and let the other person save face. Use eye contact and call people by their name. Use encouragement and make it seem easy to correct mistakes. If you are wrong, admit it. Initiate the connection. As a leader, it is your responsibility.

Listening

Listening is a skill that does not receive a lot of attention or training when we are growing up. In school, we are taught reading, writing and arithmetic, but not listening. Listening requires emotional strength, patience, openness, and the desire to understand. If you sit back and evaluate anyone you feel is a good leader, you will probably come to the realization that he is perceived to be a good listener as well.

Active listening is a developmental skill that we must learn. Most of our communication (70%-75%) is verbal communication. We spend about nine percent of time with written communication. Reading takes up about sixteen percent of communication process. We spend thirty percent of our time speaking and forty-five percent of our time listening. Studies that have been done, indicate that

If they could have, they already would have

we as humans are poor listeners. The reason for this is that we have poor listening habits and we have developed many road blocks to effective listening. Listening is hard work and requires dedication and energy. Effective listening may be the most crucial factor in an effective feedback process. There are set principles that are needed to be a good listener. Remember that humans were given two ears but only one mouth. Listening requires two ears – one used for meaning and one for feelings.

L	Look with your eyes to pick up on body language
I	Investigate; if you do not understand something, seek additional clarification
S	Suppress your reactions and/or opinions, it is not your time to speak yet
T	Tune in and stay the course, do not switch to thinking about your reply
E	Use empathy to truly understand what the person is feeling
N	Nourish a safe environment

If they could have, they already would have

Listen

*When I ask you to listen to me
And you start giving advice
You have not done what I asked.*

*When I ask you to listen to me
And you begin to tell me why I shouldn't feel that way,
You are trampling on my feelings.*

*When I ask you to listen to me
And you feel you have to do something to solve my problem,
You have failed me, strange as that may seem.*

*Listen! All I asked, was that you listen.
Not talk or do – just hear me.
Advice is cheap: 10 cents will get you both Dear Abby and
Billy Graham in the same newspaper.
And I can do for myself; I'm not helpless.
Maybe discouraged and faltering, but not helpless.*

*When you do something for me that I can and need to do
For myself, you contribute to my fear and weakness.*

*But, when you accept as a simple fact that I do feel what I feel,
No matter how irrational, then I can quit trying to convince
You and can get about the business of understanding what's
Behind this irrational feeling.*

*And when that's clear, the answers are obvious and
I don't need advice.
Irrational feelings make sense when we understand what's
Behind them.*

*Perhaps that's why prayer works, sometimes, for people
Because God is mute, and he doesn't give advice or
Try to fix things. "They" just listen and let you work it
out for yourself.*

*So, please listen and just hear me. And if you want to
Talk, wait a minute for your turn; and I'll listen to you.*

Anonymous

If they could have, they already would have

Are You a Good Listener?

Using the test below, rate your listening skills. Answer each question by circling the number that most accurately describes your assessment. Once complete, add all the numbers up for a combined total score at the bottom. Your score will reflect you listening category of excellent, good, or fair, which will allow you to focus your improvement efforts.

Assessment Area	Almost Always	Usually	Occasionally	Seldom	Almost Never
ATTITUDES					
Do you like to listen to other people talk?	5	4	3	2	1
Do you encourage other people to talk?	5	4	3	2	1
Do you listen even if you do not like the person who is talking?	5	4	3	2	1
Do you listen equally well whether the person talking is a man or a woman, young or old?	5	4	3	2	1
Do you listen equally well to friend, acquaintance, stranger?	5	4	3	2	1

If they could have, they already would have

Do you ignore clothes or general appearance?	5	4	3	2	1
ACTIONS					
Do you put what you have been doing out of mind?	5	4	3	2	1
Do you look at the person speaking?	5	4	3	2	1
Do you ignore the distractions around you?	5	4	3	2	1
Do you smile, nod your head, and otherwise encourage the person to talk?	5	4	3	2	1
Do you think about what the person is saying?	5	4	3	2	1
Do you try to figure out why the person is talking?	5	4	3	2	1
Do you let the person finish what they are trying to say?	5	4	3	2	1
If the person hesitates, do you encourage them to go on?	5	4	3	2	1
Do you re-state what the person has said and ask if you got it right?	5	4	3	2	1

If they could have, they already would have

Do you withhold judgment about the person's idea until they have finished?	5	4	3	2	1
Do you listen regardless of the person's manner of speaking and choice of words?	5	4	3	2	1
Do you listen even though you anticipate what the person is going to say?	5	4	3	2	1
Do you question the person in order to get them to explain their idea more fully?	5	4	3	2	1
Do you ask the person what particular words mean when you are unsure of the intended message?	5	4	3	2	1

Total Score_____

90-100 = Excellent Listener – continue to hone your skills

80-89 = Good Listener – investigate areas for improvement

70-79 = Fair Listener – delve into weak listening areas and develop an active listening plan.

If they could have, they already would have

Chapter 4

Outstanding Attracts Outstanding

In all our decades of working in a wide variety of industries, we have found this one truth to be self-evident. *Outstanding attracts outstanding.* If you have a top-performing, award-winning organization or office or school, people want to be on that winning team. It also works the opposite way: Outstanding repels mediocrity. People who are looking for an "easy buy" on the performance platform will shy away from outstanding organizations. They intuitively realize the amount of work and level of effort that goes into staying on the top. They do not choose to sign up for that level of effort. They may feel they will not be worthy and will not want to deal with the rejection.

The bottom line is that once you have created an outstanding organization, it will be easier to recruit and retain the cream-of-the crop people. That does not mean that staying on top will be easy, but at least one aspect of the job, attracting quality candidates, will be easier.

To reach the top or pinnacle, it is essential that you understand people. The adage, "People are your greatest asset," it really is true. There are numerous books and theories out that explain how people tick. We have read many of them and find that they all have some solid truths. The problem is that people are far too complicated to fit into a set of rules that someone sets out at a single point in time. Your educational journey toward understanding people should always be evolving and changing.

If they could have, they already would have

If you doubt this, think of the values and ethics differences between people from the Baby Boomer era and those from Generation X. The techniques designed to motivate, discipline, or reward these two groups is the difference between night and day.

In our quest to understand people, we have found that there are seven things you need to know about human beings. In embracing these seven beliefs you can build your understanding of how to work with and work for people in any environment.

Seven Things to Know About People –

- ➢ People are insecure.
- ➢ People get discouraged.
- ➢ People need to be understood.
- ➢ People want to feel special.
- ➢ People need direction.
- ➢ People want to be associated with success.
- ➢ People seek models to follow (emulate).

So you did not inherit an award-winning department or organization? Welcome to the crowd. It is very rare that you enter into an organization that is operating at its top potential. If it is, celebrate and get back to work quickly because it will not stay that way for long. Organizations are not static; they are always evolving and changing as people come and go or the market changes or the policies and procedures from your higher headquarters change. A static process always deteriorates. If not managed continuously, an organization, like a process, will devolve

If they could have, they already would have

into a state of chaos and will return to the path of least resistance.

Have you ever heard the saying, "Doing more with less?" That has become a mainstay of the Unites States military in the past decade. It has reached the point where people are now saying, "Doing less with less." The realities of draw downs and budget cuts are something that we must deal with and carry on. If this is not handled well, it will result in frustration and fear in your workplace and people will react at a very visceral level. Their basic survival may be at stake. *Good people will leave because they can.* In contrast, in uncertain times, bad people will stay because they cannot leave. Great organizations will always snatch up good people. The hardest of times are the best of times for great people. Organizations will become choosier during their hiring processes, because they can.

The people who want to be the best, who want to give the best they have to give, who want the organization to be better, who want it to be part of a well-oiled machine, who want to have an impact, and who have great ideas, want someone to listen to and appreciate them. If you do not, they will find another place that will. If they see you lowering the standards to the lowest common denominator because you think that is all you are going to get, do not be surprised. Good people will leave because they can! There are organizations around the world looking for good people: looking for innovation, imagination, opportunities for self-motivation, and high expectations! These people are dying to make a difference in the world and are going to keep moving around until they find an organization that rewards and cherishes them. So why not let it be yours?

If they could have, they already would have

PCS Syndrome

When loyal people decide to leave an organization, it generally does not happen on the spur of the moment. There are psychological stages and coping mechanisms through which they travel to prepare themselves to disassociate from the organization. In the military when employees are required to change locations or perform a Permanent Change of Station (PCS), they too will go through this mental process to help prepare them for the change. They find fault with things at the old base and tell themselves the new base will be better. We have fondly nicknamed this coping mechanism the *PCS Syndrome*. It enables the worker to justify his decision to leave and soften the requirement to move.

The stages of PCS Syndrome are:

- Disillusion
- Disgust
- Distrust
- Distance
- Departure

Disillusion

It starts out with the inability to let the day-to-day stressors die and fade away. Negative comments become more and more biting, and it is obvious that the person is not reacting in her usual get-it-done fashion. Whatever the situation, a *disillusioned* person starts seeing the glass half empty instead of seeing it half full. If a fully competent employee

If they could have, they already would have

starts to exhibit signs of disillusionment, it is the first warning sign.

When a person hits the disillusion phase, you might hear comments such as, "I can't believe that the Pentagon has sent down another task that is due today and we just got it. Look, the email chain was started two days ago, why are we just getting it now?"

"Here we go again, change 52. Guess some new commander is trying to make a name for himself and disguising it under an improvement effort."

"This is the same hurry-up-and-wait drill we did last quarter; why do they not just read the last report we sent them?"

Disgust

The *disgust* phase starts to be evident when the person gets overtly angry at the organization and leadership. He feels helpless to make things better. Already disillusioned, he now gets cynical and perhaps even spiteful about how things are run in the company. Maybe this is not outwardly apparent to all, but the indicators are there. If left unchecked, his feeling of helplessness will evolve into disgust. You may hear comments such as: "This place is so jacked; I wonder who let the monkeys loose?"

"I cannot believe that we cannot do that anymore; we have always done that before. Guess they want us to roll over and play dead."

If they could have, they already would have

Distrust

As the cycle continues, the employees feel unprotected and feel that management or the organization is no longer taking care of them. They begin to *distrust* everyone and everything. They begin to be engulfed in a dense, blanketing malaise. Helplessness is paramount; paranoia soon follows. You will hear, "Why are they not allowing us to hire vacant positions now? They probably are going to have a layoff soon."

"The boss said she would look into it, but I do not expect to hear anything back."

"Who died and left him in charge?"

Distance

The employee will start to shield her emotions and distance herself from the day-to-day decisions and operations. She no longer volunteers to serve on extra committees or get involved in anything that is not directly tied to her primary duties. She is mentally removing herself from the organization, so that the pain of departure will be bearable. You might hear, "Whatever."

"Bring it on! You can only get so much blood from this turnip in an 8-hour day."

"That's not my job."

If they could have, they already would have

Departure

Finally, the employee turns in a resignation letter. In a lot of cases, the first time the boss even realizes the person was unhappy and wishing to leave is when it is too late. He may have gotten a call from a prospective employer looking for a reference, or the person turned in his two-week notice. Since this is a Golden Child employee, the supervisor immediately shifts to the goodbye stage, saying, "Congratulations, I know you will do great things at XYZ just as you did here. When do you want to schedule your going-away luncheon?" Too often no thought is given to the reason why that person wanted to leave.

It is easy to assume that the worker is moving on to bigger and better things, such as more money, or more authority, but generally when that is the case with good employees, you know about it ahead of time and usually had a hand in steering them in that direction. When the departure comes as a surprise, it is time to look inward and see if you could have seen the PCS Syndrome building. Could you have stopped the employee from leaving?

PCS Syndrome is a symptom of an underlying de-motivating factor. There is something else going on in the mind of the employee. The first line supervisor has the best chance to find out what is going on and to keep a great employee on board.

If they could have, they already would have

Motivation

"Good people will leave because they can!"

What *motivates* a person to do a great job or even stay at a place of employment varies from person to person. Unlike popular belief, money is not the number one motivator. People are motivated differently...some are motivated by time off; some by recognition--such as receiving a thank-you, or a certificate of appreciation, or a military award. Others are motivated by promotions to a new position of authority, a position of respect, or a position of control. If someone is motivated by money, it is more than likely linked to what he can spend it on, such as grandkids, college, big toys (a boat, car, etc.) or travel. You will need to understand what motivates your people to be able to influence them.

As mentioned above, good people will leave because they can, but also bad people will stay because they can. Bad people are those employees who suck the energy out of the organization. They get by doing the minimum and will happily let others pull their weight for them. If not held accountable to higher standards of productivity, they will stay in the organization as long as the organization will let them. (The actions necessary to combat this type of behavior are covered in the Chapter 2 in the Insubordinate section.)

What is important for all of us to understand is that job security is inside of *you*, not in an organization. It is in your character, your work ethic, and your core values.

If they could have, they already would have

The list of the United States Army Core Values is one way to define internal character. They are:

- Loyalty
- Duty
- Respect
- Selfless service
- Honor
- Integrity
- Personal courage

The United States Air Force Core Values are another way to define how to conduct yourself:

- Integrity first
- Service before self
- Excellence in all we do

Whether or not a person or organization has taken the formal step to define his or its core values, most good people will already have these values embedded in their character.

I would like to tell you about my personal experience of de-motivation as it related to my own case of PCS Syndrome.

I had been in my position for too long and was openly looking for the next big adventure. My boss was well aware of my desires and was helping me with recommendations and referrals; however, at one point it

If they could have, they already would have

became apparent to me that the needs of the one did not outweigh the needs of the many.

My boss said, "Let's slow-roll your departure so you can train the new commanders who are coming in to replace the other vacant commander positions."

Did he not realize how that felt to me? I felt as though I was the second-class citizen in a supporting role and had just received 2nd place in a two-person race! It would have been much better if I had heard him say, "I need your help! Can you stay a little while longer to help me?"

The Air Force core value of Service before Self is one to which I aspire, but it sure took some internalization to get over that chat we had. I felt I had done my duty and done it well. I could even put a price tag on it: the loss of $150,000 in take-home pay over the last five years, since I had accepted a reserve position that was a lower grade because they needed my help. I had to wonder when "Service before Self" becomes "Doormat Idiot!" When does "valued" become "taken for granted?" I was very aware of these feelings and also very aware that my boss was missing all the signs of my PCS Syndrome.

Being intuitively aware of your organization and your people is essential. You need to not only be able to spot the problems areas but also recognize the great things. So how do you have an outstanding organization, one in which your employees are truly empowered? In the purest sense, the definition is easy. You tell them what to do, not how to do it. Empowerment is the way to improve quality, productivity, and employee satisfaction. This theory is absolutely true, but very difficult to implement consistently over time.

Empowerment

In a world-class organization, everybody in the company has to be thinking every day about ways to make the business better in quality, output, costs, sales and customer satisfaction. The successful organizations will be the ones best able to apply the creative energy of individuals toward constant improvement. This is *empowerment.*

The catch is that in many organizations, empowerment does not exist. The roles are set up in tiers. Upper level come up with the plans of what to do, middle level figures out how to do it and the employees carry out the work. Is that not how we have been trained? Is that not what we are getting paid for as managers and supervisors?

I am not the first to challenge this paradigm and I will not be the last; however, I feel strongly that this is one area that really needs challenging. It is not enough to pay someone well, provide good benefits or make sure she has safe working conditions. Sooner or later that employee will feel that something is missing. As supervisors and managers you need to start to question yourself and wonder what you missed.

Recovering the Negative People – They Are Worth It!

The influences that form the human psyche and motivation start far back in childhood. What exactly determines if a person grows up to be a positive person or a negative

If they could have, they already would have

person, for example? What do you do with the negative person you find on your team?

First, you have to acknowledge that negative people are not born that way! They are raised and grown into negative beings.

How do you grow negative people? Below is the evolution of a negative person:

- As a toddler:
  "Mommy, Mommy, look at my picture."
  "Not now, baby, I have to do laundry, dishes, work, etc."

- As a grade-schooler:
  "Teacher, teacher, look at my paper."
  "Not now, kid, I've got 30 other rug rats to deal with."

- As a junior high school student:
  "Can I join your clique?"
  "Uh, Duh, I don't think so!" (Derisive snicker.)

- As a high school student:
  "Can I be on the team?"
  "Nope, gotta win the championship! Need only the best and that ain't you!"

- As an 18-year-old on his first job:
  "Hey, boss, I have an idea."
  "I don't pay you to think; shut up and get back to work."

If they could have, they already would have

After enough beat-downs, the individual finally says, "Screw them! I will just keep all my great ideas to myself." Even worse, they become a negative influence in the organization, saying things like, "Hey, don't bother telling anybody your good ideas; they won't listen."

These people can be recovered, but it takes a lot of energy and time to build trust! I decided to find out what it would cost to recover a very bright, but very negative employee.

The answer is "Fifty cents!" It took fifty cents (and some nudging) to recover a negative employee and empower her to get back into the game. I asked a negative lady in our office to borrow fifty cents for a Coke, just until after lunch when I could get some change. She was confused, but she loaned it to me. I paid her back a few hours later.

The next week I asked her, "What do you think of this idea I have for a project?" She listened, and grunted, "It's okay."

A week later I asked her, "Do you have any ideas about what I was working on?"

She hesitated, but said, "I will think about it." The next day she came back with a very small idea. I incorporated her idea into the project and showed her that I had done it.

Another week went by and I asked, "Would you like to look over my project and give me some feedback?"

She took the project and immediately started looking it over. She came back with some great ideas for improvement. I incorporated all of them and gave her

If they could have, they already would have

credit in front of her peers for her contributions. For the next few weeks I carefully orchestrated our staff meetings so that she was always asked her opinion and she provided useful input each time.

In the past, she would have made denigrating comments about everyone else's ideas and snide remarks loudly enough for everyone to hear. Everyone had learned to ignore her comments. She never voiced her own opinions. She was a superstar hiding in plain sight disguised as a negative employee.

I began to take her with me to other organizations within our company when I was working a new project. I brought her as an equal collaborator and she began to provide more and more ideas. I always gave her credit to the outside organizations and to the people in our own unit. She began to cover those meetings when I was unavailable. I began to receive excellent feedback about her from those meetings.

After about 18 months, the company faced a huge layoff. Units were able to take the best and brightest from throughout the company before the layoff names were announced. Three other units asked for her by name. She was the first person placed in another organization when our section was downsized. When she came to say goodbye, she told me that she would always remember the fifty cents. She realized, and appreciated, exactly what I had done, and why I had done it.

If they could have, they already would have

Chapter 5
Improvement and Organization...
One Team at a Time

There is no such thing as a quick fix! You have to build a systematic approach and a process through which professional and personal development is sponsored throughout the chain of command, from the first line supervisor to middle management and up to the CEO. If you do not have buy-in at each of these levels, your efforts will be derailed.

Leaders must do continuous assessments of their organization. There are different leadership or management techniques that will be required depending on what you find in the assessments.

Leadership from the top is critical. You have to have buy-in to let the teams do process improvements and let the recommended changes happen. Execution at the first line supervisor level is the only way it is going to happen! True impact happens on the front lines.

The key to front line success is to establish effective teams. You need to establish Learning teams and Process Improvement teams. Remember the adage that five heads are better than one? You need to gather people together who have a vested interest in the outcome. These should be people from *inside* the process, since they know what works and what does not work.

If they could have, they already would have

I remember when I once took on a new assignment. I told myself that I was not only going to fix my own squadron, but I was going to fix the entire Wing in just six months! How naive! How arrogant! My first mistake was that I said *I* was going to fix it. Fixing or improving an organization is a strategic DECISION and it cannot be made alone. The entire organizational leadership team has to decide what needs to be fixed.

The first step is to DECIDE to fix it; i.e., to acknowledge something is wrong, or that the organization is less than it can be.

Second, you have to figure out what is wrong; i.e., you must do a Root Cause Analysis (RCA) and address the true causes of the problem, not address the symptoms.

The third step is the hardest hurdle to overcome. The leadership team has to acknowledge that the problem is US! It is very hard to admit, "We are the problem."

The fourth step is to engage every level of leadership in the solutions. You have to start with round table discussions and ask each one of them:

> - "If you could change one thing, what would you change?"
> - "Why that one thing?"
> - "What is the strategic significance of that one thing?"

If they could have, they already would have

The plan to improve your organization should be more than just a good idea tossed around during a staff meeting. It needs to be based on a systematic process that is measureable and repeatable. Here are some recommended steps:

Step 1. Identify all requirements (core missions) first.

Step 2: Identify resources needed to meet these requirements. If necessary, fight for the scare resources, such as manpower, equipment, computers and time.

Step 3. Identify and document the processes required to meet the requirements.

Step 4. Think deeply about how you will know you are meeting the requirements and identify metrics to measure this. Track and check the metrics against goals weekly or periodically. This process needs to be cyclical, where you go back to the planning stage and check what has been accomplished against what has been measured to ensure it is on track. This cycle is called the PDCA: Plan, Do, Check and Act. Word of warning: you need to look for efficiencies, but always stay focused on effectiveness! Effectiveness means that the process is achieving the required results. A process can be so efficient that you lose effectiveness.

Step 5. Organizational change that is going to stick requires the best possible leadership team. This may require some hard reviews and possible removal of the previous leadership team. You have to remind yourself,

If they could have, they already would have

"If they could have, they already would have." It is important that they be removed, not just moved around. Start by clearly assessing middle and first line people to see if they have had good leadership. The success factor is really about leadership.

Step 6. It is now time to give your unit an honest report card (A-F) to see where your strengths and weaknesses lie. Look at recent inspections, audits or staff assistance visits for a baseline assessment.

F – Program Failure. If you find program failures than rate yourself an F in those areas. Prioritize these "critical failures" and fix those first. Build a one-to-three year improvement plan. Realistically, in most large organizations, it will take up to three years. This is the time to rally the troops and remind them, "One team, one fight!" Leadership is truly key here. You need strong, knowledgeable people who can help guide others. You need leaders who can accelerate the knowledge of the employees. A good leader can jump start them at 60 percent baseline, not from zero.

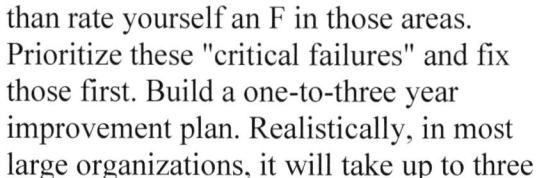

D- Status Quo. If you are below minimum standards, then rate yourself as a D. This is the time for leadership to focus on processes. You need to integrate your people into the equation through empowerment. Your focus should be with the first line supervisors. You need a point of contact (POC) to "honcho" each program. If you are successful, your people will take ownership. You need to let them run with it! Run with new ideas and technology. You cannot abandon the programs or the people. You have to use a systematic review of metrics so you can stay on top of the gains. And more importantly, hold those gains! During your assessment process, bring in Staff Assistant Visits (SAVs) from outside organizations every year. Conduct self-inspections at least two times a year. Train your people in the Continuous Improvement Processes (CIPs) to help them sustain, refine, and improve processes within programs. Reward success, especially successful CIP projects. Reward innovation! You need to empower the younger generation, since they are light years ahead in terms of technology and we all need to work smarter, not harder. Challenge them to figure this out.

    C – Should Be. If you are meeting minimum standards, then rate yourself as a C. If all programs are just meeting minimum organizational standards and customer requirements, then you are just an average organization. Your competition will easily overtake you in the market. At this rating, you will be carrying about three to five percent mediocre employees. The de-motivational factor created by these employees on others has a multiplier effect of ten to 15 percent reduced productivity. Dead weight employees will only slow you down and bring down the momentum of others. Accountability is key, and if missing, will de-motivate your high potential employees (HIPOTs). Your HIPOTs want to work hard, but are not interested in carrying the workload of mediocre employees. In this environment, good people will leave, because they can.

If they could have, they already would have

B – Could Be. Give yourself a B grade if your programs are all rated above average when compared against your peers or organizational standards. Leaders need to carefully assess employee performance at least quarterly to ensure that they keep on track and are focused on the right things. Your continuous feedback and discipline are crucial. Use a sharp knife as needed and keep only the best employees on hand. The leader's job is to focus on training opportunities, inculcate policy changes (with employee input), keep an eye on low performers, document performance, look for and remove mediocrity. Do not preach accountability; enforce it! Last, look for ways to reward HIPOTs and find ways to expand their empowerment levels. Leader's job should be to identify and prioritize mission requirements, provide resources, remove barriers (even if it is you!), promote and encourage rewards and recognition, and inspire to greatness.

A – Greatness! Your organization is rated an A if you are the role model for others, i.e., the benchmark. Now it is all about staying out of the way! Wind them up and let them loose! You need to ensure every layer of the organization is on track by using reliable metrics. Ensure that you have systematic approaches to every process. Do not take your eye off the ball for even a minute. Set up your internal audits, Staff Assistance Visits and self-inspections, and lock them in. Look for new missions and customers. Remember that growth management is linear, not exponential. Unless you discover the next worldwide new thing, like Bill Gates or Steve Jobs did, your growth should be steady and linear in most cases. Teach others. Build Centers of Excellence. Be known as the role model;

be your own Public Affairs office and market your organization. Build your reputation. Go help others; be on Staff Assistance Visit teams to other agencies. The best way to learn is to teach! Listen, look, and steal ideas while you are there.

Ask yourself, "Why not here?" Why not stop right now and say, "How about now? How about right here in this place, in this organization? Why can we not be the "Center of Excellence?"

If they could have, they already would have

Chapter 6

Career Cycles

You and your employees should change jobs every three-to-five years! Definitely stay in place no more than five years; any longer than that and you and the organization will stagnate. If you stay in the same exact job longer than five years, the job and the organization will wear you down into static conformity. You will be subverted into organizational cultural norms. That is not good for your personal growth or for the organization.

The three-year cycle is optimal. In the first year you should focus on learning and executing the job. Become the subject matter expert! The second year you should be looking at fine-tuning and improving the programs and processes. In the third year you should be training your replacement. You want to build the bench so you can move on, guilt-free, and leave the organization better off than you found it! Put your "heir apparent(s)" into learning opportunities whenever possible, such as while you are away on vacation or business travel. Design them a set of training opportunities which allow them to grow into their duties and responsibilities. They will be eager to take the reins and you will be free for your next big adventure.

If you stay more than five years in the same job, what are you really doing? Are you blocking the next generation? They will become discontented waiting for you to get out of the way. You move into an 8-to-5 mentality. You feel

If they could have, they already would have

like you are just putting in time. If you do not keep moving, you personally and professionally degrade. The mission degrades. You become complacent. You stop looking for process improvement opportunities because you just want to do your job and want everyone else to leave you alone. You have already fixed everything, so you have difficulty doing continuous improvement with your own processes, something you have created. You do not see the forest for the trees. It is time to move!

How do you know when it is time to leave a job? That is simple: When you have learned everything you were supposed to learn, and when you have taught everything you were supposed to teach.

Sometimes learning and improving your job will take two years each. That is when the cycle stretches to five years. But at five years, it is time to move up and out of the job. If you do not go, you are now officially homesteading. It is time to move out of the way for the next generation. It is time for a new opportunity to grow and learn for both you and your replacement.

The world is changing way too fast; we have to do more with less; we have to stay on top of technological changes and put the technology to good use. By homesteading you are not doing yourself or the organization any favors, and you are definitely not serving the people coming behind you!

Most importantly, you need to take personal responsibility for your own career. I was a fifteen-year Staff Sergeant in

If they could have, they already would have

the Air Force. For fifteen years I stagnated in one rank. In my own mind, I was a "super troop." I was smart; I was an A-student in college. I had my Master's degree, my Bachelor's and my Associate degrees. In my own mind, I was a wonderful employee. But the reality did not support my mindset. How did I stay a Staff Sergeant for fifteen years if I was so wonderful? In reality, I was an arrogant, snot-nosed, holier-than-thou, know-it-all snob! I did not have a clue about when to shut up.

My ex-husband used to say to me all the time, "For someone so smart, you are so stupid!" Needless to say, I did not want to hear that, but he was right. I had the book smarts, but I was self-sabotaging every day! My goal should have been to exude humble confidence, but I did not have a clue about humble confidence at that time in my life. You cannot do false humility, because it is fake and insincere. No one is fooled.

For true professional success, you have to have confidence in your knowledge. You can prove yourself to others by quoting regulation and sources, whether it is a civilian research paper or a regulation in the military environment. You have to be the "go-to" person. As you do this, you build up self-confidence and credibility, which leads people to trust you and what you say, which leads to recognition for your capabilities. But this knowledge has to be provided to others in a humble, helpful way. It does not matter what you know if no one will listen.

If they could have, they already would have

Manage Your Own Career

To *manage your career*, you have to lead from wherever you sit! Whether you are at the bottom tier or the top tier, or anywhere in the middle, you can lead from wherever you sit.

Leadership looks like this:

- "Ma'am, I have an idea."
- "Sir, I think I have a better way to do that."
- "Sir, I think we can save a thousand dollars a day by making this one change."
- "Ma'am, may I volunteer to help you on that project?"

It is not about taking over or taking control, or stepping outside your lane or usurping someone else's leadership; it is about sharing your knowledge, sharing your ideas, volunteering to assist and proving yourself over time. A student told me that his boss told him, "Play your career like a game of chess not like a game of checkers."

Most importantly, you have to take personal responsibility for your own career. If you are not being promoted, or you are not being recognized, you need to go out and seek feedback to find out why. You have to ask someone, "What am I doing wrong? What else could I be doing?" You need to seek out mentors.

If they could have, they already would have

Mentors

You should have a minimum of two *mentors*. The first mentor should be your first-line supervisor. That is the person who ought to be telling you if what you are doing is working or not. Are you being productive? Are you accomplishing the organizational goals? Those two things are the minimum of what you need to know. You have to be successful in what you have been hired to do before you go looking for other opportunities. First and always, you have to do your job! That is what the organization is paying you to do. Your managers need you to do it and to do it well!

The second mentor is someone who has done or is doing what you want to do. You need to think about what you want to be when you grow up. What career field do you want to be in? Then go find a person that has already done that. Ask her how she did it. What changes did she make? How often did she change jobs? What education did she achieve? What professional organizations did she join?

For example, if you are an enlisted person and you want to be an officer, go find someone who has made that transition! You need to find someone who has done it well, who is highly respected; and let him explain to you how it works. If you want to go from a non-flying position to a flying position, go find someone who has done that. Go find someone who is emulating and living your dream and talk to him. Ask him, "How did you do that?" "What should I be doing to make myself more marketable and to

If they could have, they already would have

make that transition?" "What should I be doing to position myself to do what I want to do someday, i.e., to get to a particular success in the future?" "What are the building blocks I need to be putting in place today?"

Above all, YOU must take personal responsibility for your career and your success. First-line supervisors can barely take care of their own careers, so do not wait for someone else to say, "You are wonderful! We should promote you, but here is what you have to do for that to happen."

If they could have, they already would have

Chapter 7

Senior Leaders

Let me start out by stating the obvious. Leaders must lead! Yep, it is right there in the name, *Lead*ership. Leading is not the problem, though. The hard part is finding where to lead or to what end.

No matter what type of job we hold, all leaders have a similar job description. The job description of a leader is to:

- ➢ Establish the vision
- ➢ Set strategic policies
- ➢ Identify and prioritize mission requirements
- ➢ Provide resources
- ➢ Remove barriers
- ➢ Provide rewards and recognition
- ➢ Inspire to greatness

One thing that should be apparent to you as a leader is that you cannot do it by yourself. You need your employees marching with you. Four of the most powerful words a leader can say are, "I need your help!"

If they could have, they already would have

Mission First--People Always

Strategic Policies

The single most important responsibility for a senior leader is to develop *strategic policies* for both the organization and the people. This cannot be delegated. Senior leaders must own the concept of the mission first. The middle management team and first line supervisor own people always. In a military situation, the award of command authority to a single leader ultimately establishes the delineation of ownership. In a civilian organization, this command authority resides with the CEO. The levels below command authority own the equitable application of strategic-level business and personnel policies.

Senior leaders look at strategic policies from the 30,000 foot (as if up in an aircraft) viewpoint. Middle management views the organization from the 500-foot level, and first line supervisors view the organization from ground level. Leaders at all levels must find the balance between meeting the needs of the mission (profit) and the needs of the people. Variations in the execution and implementation of policies occur due to the view of each leader. Front line supervisors may interpret and execute policies differently than originally intended by the senior leadership. There must be checks and balances put into place, therefore, to provide oversight to enforce the policies equitably.

Here is an example of equitability. As a member of the Wing Executive Council (WEC), I participated in

If they could have, they already would have

conducting Standards of Discipline meetings to ensure consistent execution of policies across the entire organization. In one case, there was a male member charged with sexual assault in the civilian court system. There would be no military jurisdiction, so for expediency, we essentially allowed the member to retire to get him off the base as soon as possible. In this case, he would be eligible for retirement benefits. In another case, occurring at the same time in another subordinate organization, a member was recommended for discharge for cause because he was over the military weight standards. If discharged, he would lose his retirement benefits. Both agencies were operating within the established personnel policies, yet the results would not be equitable. The person accused of assault would collect his retirement while another who was merely overweight would forfeit his retirement benefits.

When this inequity was revealed during the senior-level policy review, the Wing Commander halted the separation for the overweight member. The member was allowed to retire with full benefits.

An unexpected consequence to this strategic decision was that the supervisor of the overweight member felt undermined. The supervisor lost his motivation to ever work that hard again on a personnel action. It takes a lot of time, effort and documentation to separate/fire someone for cause. If the decision was going to be overturned at the senior level anyway, why should he work that hard?
In this scenario, the first line supervisor lost the energy to hold people accountable at the ground level of the

If they could have, they already would have

organization. Middle management had to work closely with the front line supervisor to mitigate the long-term effects that would be caused by a lack of accountability at the ground level.

Following the rules without having the macro view of what was going on in the larger organization, however, could also have been devastating to the organizational culture. If the overweight person had lost his retirement while the sex offender had gotten his full benefits, members throughout the organization would have seen the results as unfair and would have lost trust in senior leadership.

Seeking this balance between strategic and ground-level execution falls under the auspices of the art of leadership. In both cases, there were clearly established personnel policies. Only when viewed from the strategic level were the personnel actions at odds with each other.

Strategic policies must be written to capture the eighty-percent solution. If you consider a bell curve, a well-written policy will cover the center of the curve and will apply to 80 percent of personnel cases. The above two instances fell outside the bell curve and needed to be considered as special cases. There will be people on either side of the curve; some on the far left who are deserving of immediate discipline and separation, and some on the far right who may have medical problems and require personalized dispensation. Don't try to write macro policies to meet 100 percent of all cases; you will never succeed. Instead, handle special cases with an oversight committee.

If they could have, they already would have

The answer to every special case develops the cultural norm for how to handle this case in the future. If many of the same special cases occur, the policy will move into the bell curve and no longer require a special solution. The solution becomes the precedent for future situations with similar components.

People Issues

People issues are the most time-consuming and the most critical actions required of leaders. Some of these issues can only be handled by senior leaders. If the organizational culture is one where people are moved around instead of fired, only the most senior leader can break that cultural norm.

When I joined one particular organization, it was a disaster! It was run like a country club, not a military organization. Upon review of my manning document, I found 85 authorized positions in the organization. Three of these were full-time positions and the rest were traditional Guard slots in which members had to perform duty one weekend each month. The reality was that I had 44 vacancies and only 38 names listed on the manning document. Nine of these names were people who were no longer showing up for duty and needed to be removed from the personnel roster. Another twelve were what I considered "malignant" members and were a cancer to our unit. Only seventeen members were productive and dedicated to the mission of the organization.

If they could have, they already would have

My first step was to come up with the plan to remedy this manpower fiasco.

I immediately completed the necessary administrative paperwork to remove the non-participating personnel from our manning document to open up their positions so they could be recruited. The next step was to identify personnel options for removing the "malignancies" through separations, retirements, or transfers to other units that could better use their talents. Simultaneously, I worked with the recruiters and prioritized their efforts based on our critical personnel needs. Once gained, I purposely placed the new recruits in a different building away from the malignant members. I did not want the new members tainted by the old country club culture.

Next I did the necessary due diligence to remove two full-time employees for cause. One member was unwilling to perform her duties, and the other was incapable of performing the required duties. It took a long time and a ton of documentation to remove these members. First, I had to convince my senior leadership that the employees should be removed, not just moved around, which went against the previous cultural norm. I replaced them with high performers who hit the ground running at the highest standards of performance.

All of these efforts to clean house required a huge amount of commander involvement and micro-managing. Unfortunately, I spent so long in the "fix it" mode that I failed to realize when it was finally fixed and continued to

127

If they could have, they already would have

micro-manage. I had hired the best but was not allowing them to perform with minimal supervision.

I forgot to change my modus operandi once I had changed the organization! I kept treating people like the losers I first encountered when I took over the organization, not the high-performing team I had put together. I kept over-controlling and hammering people to raise their standards when they were already there. I had begun to demotivate them before I realized the obvious. Thankfully, we had built a high trust environment among the new employees so I was able to get the feedback I so sorely needed.

A couple of my front-line employees had the courage and commitment to come and talk to me. They told me, "You are the problem, ma'am. People want to leave because of you!" I was shocked and hurt, but then I realized they were right. Once I "fixed" the organization, I forgot to move from fixing into empowering. Thank goodness for employees with the personal courage to come forward. I would have lost everything I had worked so hard to build.

Get in the KAR!

To build or maintain an outstanding organization, you have to have all your employees riding in the same car, heading in the same direction, toward the same vision. The problem is that *people do not know what they do not know.* That silly little statement is the great "Aha!" for an effective leader.

If they could have, they already would have

For us, this realization was the answer to all our strategic alignment questions. These questions include, "Why do we have to do strategic planning; is it not a wasted exercise?" "Why do our goals need to mirror or complement the division above us; we have our own job to do?" "We know our job; why can we not just do it?"

Then the light came on for us...people do not know what they do not know.

Armed with our new philosophy, we gave birth to the concept and acronym *"Get in the KAR."* The formula is K + A = R! *Knowledge plus Accountability equals Results.*

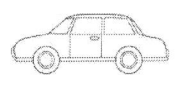

We developed this process as a means to bring all players on to the same field within the organization by using this easily repeatable phrase. We challenged them to "Get in the KAR!" We asked them, "Are you driving the KAR or are you just riding shotgun and babysitting the status quo?"

The K stands for Knowledge. It is all about gaining knowledge with a capital K--not "I think," or "I guess," but fact-based certainty used for decision-making. In a high-performance organization, all members must know their jobs, whether it is based on regulations, standard operating procedures, academic research, professional sources, or strategic policies. Seek the knowledge and the results will come.

If they could have, they already would have

But what is knowledge? It is a noun defined (in Webster's dictionary) as facts, information, and skills acquired by a person through experience or education; the theoretical or practical understanding of a subject, or the awareness or familiarity gained by experience of a fact or situation.

Synonyms for knowledge are understanding, comprehension, grasp, command or mastery. Understanding must start with knowledge! To ensure that you are using and passing on the correct knowledge you need to prepare first. This is accomplished by following the guidance in Chapter 8, which deals with getting back to basics. It is a personal journey for each employee. Take the time to look at your own level of understanding; i.e., what you really know versus what you think you know. This is a great starting point to focus your studies, and your own efforts to get back to basics."

"Light travels faster than sound. This is why some people appear bright until you hear them speak."

Unknown

How true this is. Have you ever sat in a meeting and seen someone dig a hole for himself by trying to gloss over the information he should know, or just butcher it and do the MSU?

If they could have, they already would have

Not familiar with MSU? It stands for "making stuff up," and when someone does it and tries to pull off the made-up stuff off as fact, it is not only embarrassing for them but for the others in the room as well. As you are sitting around the conference room table listening to this person stutter and stammer as she tries to explain some data point to the boss, you feel her pain. You wish that she would just shut up, acknowledge that she simply does not know, and offer to get back to the boss with the correct answer. No, she keeps digging herself into a bigger hole. The bottom line is, no MSU. Be the subject matter expert (SME). Do not merely think you have the answer--know you have the knowledge or at least know where to find the answers. Know your sources, guidelines, playbooks or whatever other directives rule your environment. Operate from the position of the capital K: If you are giving your professional opinion, then ensure that it is very clear to everyone that you are giving an OPINION, not stating a fact. Credibility is earned through your knowledge. If you get caught making stuff up, you will pay for it for à long time. It is very hard to get credibility back once it has been tarnished. This requires that you embrace continual learning because things change all the time and your current knowledge will be outdated before you know it.

When everyone has reached the step of a foundation based on knowledge, then leaders have to ensure employees have the means to accomplish the mission. Everyone should be saying, "I know what to do and I have the means to do it, check."

If they could have, they already would have

Once everyone has the K and it is moving down the road, you now have to ensure that there is accountability. A new wing commander I worked for had a very interesting distinction to obtaining his own capital K. In response to the adage that leaders should not micro-manage, he stated, "I don't want to micro-manage, I want to micro-know." His philosophy was based on the premise, "How can I lead if I don't KNOW, with a capital K?" His learning process also allowed him to gauge the trust level he felt with the knowledge of his subordinates.

Accountability

Accountability is the core component of all outstanding organizations. Everyone must hold themselves, peers, and subordinates accountable. Although you might not be able to hold your superiors accountable, each person should inform his superiors when suspected violations of rules and regulations happen. It is not always easy to tell your boss that he is the problem. It takes personal courage to do so.

This 360-degree circle of accountability keeps the organization aligned to the highest standards and performance indicators. Without accountability, there is chaos. There will be unpredictable results and discontented employees. There will be perceived favoritism and unfair practices.

Adherence to strategic policies and procedures is the cornerstone of vertical and horizontal alignment within an organization. Senior leaders must be able to trust that every layer of management is executing agreed-upon policies. This alignment ensures everyone is moving together toward the organization's vision and goals.

You are not doing people favors when you do not hold them accountable. You are training them to think that their substandard performance is acceptable. You lose your ability to expect higher levels of productivity out of them. You are telling them, "Substandard performance is the standard around here."

Accountability through feedback is intended to correct performance before it becomes the acceptable norm. Most people will respond to accountability with the right attitude and be appreciative. The few who get belligerent or defensive have underlying issues (insubordinate, incompetent, or incapable). When an employee responds favorably to accountability, be sure to tell her how impressed you are with her mature responsiveness. This will go a long way toward the employees' willingness to sustain their performance at the highest levels.

Results

If your team has knowledge and accepts and understands their accountability, then you cannot help but get *results*. The truth is you will get results regardless of your knowledge or accountability; it just will not be the results you want. What you want is predictable results or desired results. What you do not want is unpredictable results or happenstance.

If they could have, they already would have

Predictable results involve getting the job done right the first time; all players having the same end in mind; everyone marching to the same drummer; projects on time and on budget; and a feeling of job satisfaction among all team members.

Unpredictable results create re-work; missed deadlines; unmet objectives; misunderstandings or misconceptions; finger-pointing and blaming; exceeded budgets; and massive amounts of frustration for everyone.

In a military medical unit, one of the missions is to ensure that all military members of the Wing are fit for duty. This process involves an annual physical exam for all 1,200 members assigned. When I took over one such unit, we were getting dismal results. Our annual physical exam completion rate was 49 percent. The national goal was 82 percent. The medical organization had very low credibility and other commanders were reluctant to support our exam process. When they would send their people to our appointments, they would lose them for the whole day due to poor time utilization. The commanders could not afford to lose their people for eight hours so they elected not to send them at all.

We also had a terrible reputation for having incorrect data. So, my first job was to instill into the medical unit members that our only source of credibility is accurate data! Once we gained credibility about our data (and quit losing paperwork), we then focused on improving our internal processes.

If they could have, they already would have

It was only after we cleaned up our own internal processes that we could seek a partnership with the other commanders. To ensure that their people would come to their appointments, I made a deal with the commanders. I told them, "Send your people to me and I will get them current (known as 'in the green') on their annual exams and back to you in less than two hours."

To live up to this promise, we used a continuous process improvement (CPI) effort to streamline our internal processes. We had to get the eight-hour physical exam process down to 1.5 hours. In the beginning our data told a sad story. Every stage in the process had excessive wait times. Everywhere you looked, you saw members hanging out, waiting to be seen. They were bored, frustrated and looking for ways to escape back to their offices.

First, I had to get all medical group members aligned with one single goal: Get people green in less than two hours! We had to begin with a root cause analysis on every one of the 18 stations in the physical exam process. We pinpointed the stages with the highest wait times and identified solutions to reduce each one. We realigned manpower, incorporated line facilitators, and staggered the appointment times. These may seem like obvious fixes, but they were critical pieces to meeting our promises.

We put into place systemic fixes to ensure that we held the gains. In partnership with the commanders, we recommended that everyone be scheduled to accomplish their exams during their birth month. This predictability made the scheduling a lot easier for us, the member, and the commanders. We marketed this process as, "A free annual physical exam for your birthday present!" This was not an easy fix; it took time and a significant effort on the part of the entire organization. However, years later we are still holding the gains. We now average an 85 percent completion rate, consistently meeting the national goal. We are also living up to the promise of completing the process in less than two hours.

Members even now call us to say, "It's my birthday month; shouldn't I be coming to see you guys?" The members have been vested in the process. We no longer have to police them or their supervisors to get them to their appointments.

Results: Efficiency vs. Effectiveness (a cautionary tale)

As you seek to improve processes and procedures, there will be a tendency to want to be as efficient as possible. Your tendency will be to seek *efficient* process improvements. There can be a significant difference, however, between effectiveness and efficiency. It can be very efficient to send an email to someone and think that your job is done; i.e., you notified them. What you may not know is whether the person received the email and understood it, or if the tone of voice within the email was irritating. Do not assume because you take the path of least resistance (i.e. send an email) that the efficient way is always the effective way. The most important aspect of any program is its effectiveness. *Effectiveness* is defined by asking these questions:

If they could have, they already would have

> Did you achieve the goal, as defined by the program's metrics? (e.g. 82%)
> Did you achieve the required results? (i.e. members are "fit to fight")
> Do you have a gap between where you are now and where you are supposed to be? (for example, 49% vs. 82%)

To tie into the illustration above, if your Individual Medical Readiness rate is 76 percent and the Air Force goal is 82 percent, it does not matter how *efficient* you are at sending emails to members telling them they have a physical exam appointment. Based on the metrics, they are obviously not being seen; therefore, you have not been *effective*. When you seek results, you need to focus on *effective* processes, not merely *efficient* processes.

When you get in the KAR, you have to be careful that you do not get so efficient that you forget about effectiveness. Once you have identified the program requirements, the resources you have, and the processes that you already have in existence, then check the metrics for effectiveness. Once you have accomplished the goal and are hitting the desired mark consistently month after month, then look inside the process and begin to "lean" it out. Look for those efficiencies where you can do it cheaper, smarter, faster, but always remain focused on effectiveness. If you are efficient but not effective, your program has failed.

Okay, so now you know about putting the mission first. Next, we will explore the "people always" concepts.

If they could have, they already would have

Know Your People

The belief that effective leaders need to know their people is not new. The current leadership lore about how to know your people deals with the whole person concept. You may feel comfortable if you know their birthdates, their hobbies, and their families' names, but knowing your people goes a lot deeper than this.

What I believe is that you must *know yourself* and how you *feel* about your people. We all bring our own prejudices and paradigms with us every day. We see others through the eyes of these internal belief systems. Without stopping to check your beliefs often, you can limit the full potential and possibilities of your employees. We all know that our people are our greatest assets, but do we really believe this? Sometimes our view of our people is clouded by what we think they should be, and we do not see their true value. A couple of stories below illustrate this inevitable challenge.

The manager of a convenience store was expressing her frustration concerning personnel issues with me. High turnover of people was a never-ending problem and considered the evil of her profession. She would get someone trained so he could work on his own, and then he would quit or just not show up for work anymore. With the pay barely above minimum wage, rotating hours and limited benefits, it was hard to keep employees for any length of time. Her training program was a vicious cycle with no end in sight.

If they could have, they already would have

This manager was also frustrated with having to deal with one employee who was a slow learner and had probably received special education during her school years. It was normal for even the simplest process to be explained to her multiple times before she could grasp it. Once she did get it, though, she would perform the task flawlessly. Her attitude was exceptional and she loved her job, which was in great contrast with some of her co-workers, who felt the job was demeaning and were waiting for something better to come along. The manager saw this worker as an additional training burden in her already strained training program. I saw this worker as her greatest asset.

I asked, "Look at your list of employees and tell me who will still be around in six months." She laughed and said, "Probably none of them. No, wait; probably only the one that I am spending extra time training."

I responded, "What would you be willing to do to keep an employee long term? Would you be willing to spend more time training that person?"

"Of course," she answered, and the light bulb came on. She was able to see this worker in a new light. When I stopped back in that store three years later, that employee's smiling face was still there to greet me.

Another situation dealt with a plant manager's frustrations in having non-native English speakers on the production line. There frequently arose miscommunication when dealing with these workers. When I brought to his attention that these were the only employees who showed up

If they could have, they already would have

consistently to work, it changed his attitude. Yes, these workers were worth the extra effort because their work ethic was priceless.

Your people are your real assets. The people who know the processes inside and out are right there in your organization! Invest in training your people on problem solving, process improvement and program management. Give them the tools and they will take care of getting you the results you need.

I experienced this last example firsthand: You are truly not a prophet in your own land. For example, when I was an independent consultant and paid significant fees, corporate leadership would listen to every word I had to say. However, if you pay me a salary and I work inside the organization, apparently I do not know anything and cannot be trusted to advise senior leadership; even though I hold the same credentials I did when I was a consultant.

We need to ask ourselves, "Didn't we hire the best-qualified people? If so, why don't we listen to them?" Why is it that we cannot teach, consult or advise inside our own organization? Why must someone leave the organization to become a million-dollar consultant and charge big bucks to be perceived as an expert?

Regardless, even if we never figure out that conundrum, the bottom line is that change does not happen from the outside in. It has to occur from the inside.

If they could have, they already would have

Change Management

The key to successful change is to illuminate the rewards of individual change; i.e., the personal victory. One's buy-in to "being the best I can be" will result in increased self-confidence, increased contribution capacity, a sense of identity, integrity, control, exhilaration and peace. We all must learn to define ourselves from within, rather than through other people's opinions or by comparison to others. This is the only way to effect true personal change.

Maslow's Hierarchy of Needs versus Organizational Hierarchy

In a conversation with a leadership team, a manager commented that people (employees) always have something to complain about. No matter how much you give employees, they always want more.

I explained this phenomenon as "raising the bar on Maslow's hierarchy of needs." The complaints brought up during the previous internal assessment dealt with the basic needs of the facility and working conditions. Now that those concerns had been met, the bar had been raised. In the latest employee survey, for example, the employees' comments were focused on wanting to feel involved in decision-making. They also did not feel treated like part of the team.

People will always find things that they want to see improved. They will work their way up Maslow's

If they could have, they already would have

hierarchy until they are self-actualized within the organization. For some people, self-actualization occurs when they believe they belong to a meaningful organization (belonging needs). Other people may need to believe their opinions are heard and appreciated (self-esteem need).

Leadership's response to their issues should be based on the hierarchy level about which the people are complaining; e.g. basic survival needs, sense of security, or belonging needs, etc.

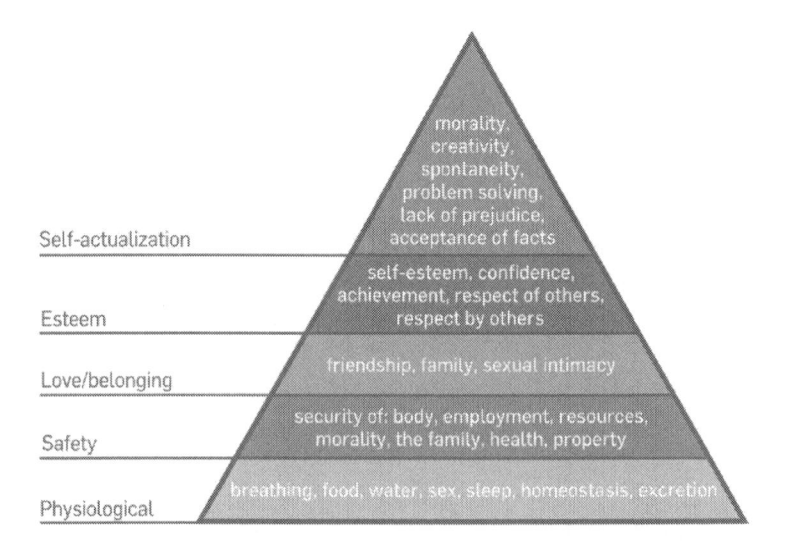

Self-actualization — morality, creativity, spontaneity, problem solving, lack of prejudice, acceptance of facts

Esteem — self-esteem, confidence, achievement, respect of others, respect by others

Love/belonging — friendship, family, sexual intimacy

Safety — security of: body, employment, resources, morality, the family, health, property

Physiological — breathing, food, water, sex, sleep, homeostasis, excretion

The manager responded after this explanation with, "Hell, I thought I just had a bunch of whiners working here."

If they could have, they already would have

The moral of the story is that if your people are not complaining or providing feedback to improve the organization, it is not that there are no complaints. Your people are telling everyone but you.

Dimensions of Leadership

There are three distinct dimensions of leadership in which we must operate: sociological, psychological and astrological (i.e. situational). Each dimension is interwoven with the others, yet requires a different level of understanding of human behavior, motivation and relationships.

Sociological

The *sociological* aspect deals with relationships. The relational issues between leaders and followers deal with interpersonal skills such as communications. The organization piece deals with culture, such as, your culture of diversity and your values.

Psychological

The *psychological* dimension deals with the person. It includes his character, abilities, experiences, and personality.

Astrological

The *astrological* dimension is situational and is impacted by what is going on in the world around us such as war, whether we are at peace, whether there is a crisis or a natural catastrophe. The astrological influences are external to the person, team and the organization as well. The influences can also be political and deal with what is happening in the country such as the impact of a sequestration and a government shutdown.

Leadership is a reciprocal relationship between those who choose to lead and those who choose to follow. Any discussion of leadership must attend to the dynamics of this relationship. Strategies, tactics, skills, and best practices are empty unless we understand the fundamental human aspirations that connect leaders and their followers.

Whatever leadership style you possess, to be successful, it must be built on trust. In addition, your organizational structure must allow some degree of autonomy and it must have flexibility and agility built in.

Responsibility

Sharing *responsibility* or delegating responsibility does not mean abandoning responsibility. A leader still has the responsibility to know what is going on, set the direction for the department, make the decisions subordinates cannot, ensure that people are on course, and offer a guiding hand. You need to open doors to clear the way, assess performance and be a smart manager.

Leadership is about influence.

If they could have, they already would have

All the leadership theory out there is true and will work, but it is harder than hell to execute consistently and to sustain over time! We all know that one "Aw, sh-t" undoes 99 "Atta-boys!"

During a major military readiness exercise, as the commander I lost my cool and started yelling orders at my people. They assumed I was mad at them since my anger appeared to be directed at them. In reality, I was livid at another organization's commander who was attempting to control my processes. After the fact, many members were threatening to leave my unit because of me! Despite five years of building and taking care of my unit through promotions, great training opportunities, additional manning and resources etc., it all came down to the one time I broke their trust and treated them as children instead of adults.

In another situation, I set up a training opportunity for my Air National Guard members in Hawaii. Great, right? Apparently not. This was seen by some as a negative thing. One member lamented being away from her full-time work for two weeks when only ten days would be paid military days. She would have to use two days of personal leave time. Others hated the field conditions in Hawaii--now there is an oxymoron! It reinforced to me that no good deed goes unpunished.

If they could have, they already would have

Unintentional Influence (Negative and Positive)

One thing leaders need to remember is that we are impacting people around us every minute of every day. They are watching what we say and what we do, and when our actions do not match our words, they always believe our actions. None of this, "Do as I say, not as I do!" will ever work. We have to be mindful of the unintentional influences that occur, such as the little faux pas that occur without even realizing the dichotomy of our actions. Let's say you lecture people to show up on time, but they hear you answer the phone and tell the caller you are in a meeting to justify being late. Your people know you are not in a meeting. This is not the picture of integrity you want them to see.

I knew a co-worker who would fib to clients all the time saying, "I'll be out of town," or "I can't make it then; I'm already booked," when she was not. When she was confronted about this behavior, she said, "It's just business." What kind of unintentional messages are we sending to our staff by doing this?

Another area of your influence encompasses the actions of those who directly report to you. Your executive officer or deputy may use your authority to carry out her own duties, because it is an easier way to get things done. Many times I have learned the hard way that this was happening. She may be telling others, "The boss wants this," but it may not be something you actually stated. You need to have a very clear understanding with your deputy or executive officer about when she can or cannot drop your name.

If they could have, they already would have

If you are very, very lucky someday, you will be told about the positive influence you had on someone's life. I have had that happen several times. Once as a faculty associate at a state university, I was teaching a section on career choices. We were discussing how to know what your gift is and that if you are able to do what you really love, it would never be work. It would be a great career.

A student walked up to me after class and said, "Ma'am, I do not really want to be an engineer. I want to be a fireman. My parents want me to be an engineer, and because they are paying for my tuition that is what I am studying. They figured that's where all the jobs are."

So I said to him, "Do your parents love you?" He looked at me, startled, and said, "Of course they do!" I said, "Then tell them exactly what you just told me."

I never heard back from him about what happened; he finished his semester with me and I did not see him again until 15 years later. I was at a bank running an errand when I saw a man wearing a fire battalion chief uniform.

He walked up to me and said, "Are you Ms. Edwards?"

I said, "Well, I used to be, a couple of marriages ago."

He said, "I took a class from you years ago."

I looked at him and said, "Oh, my God! Look at you! I do remember you! How have you been?"

If they could have, they already would have

He said, "I am a firefighter and a Battalion Chief today because of you, and I wanted to thank you. I have a wife, two children, and I love my job. I have never forgotten what you said to me that day after class."

What a blessing it was to get to know the rest of the story fifteen years later of the influence I had that day.

Another time I was working at a large helicopter manufacturing company. Eight thousand people worked there and had to go through a security checkpoint every day. The poor gate guards had to check 8,000 badges every day.

They would be constantly saying, "Would you put your badge on, please? Could you take your badge out of your pocket? Would you clip your badge above your waist please?"

All day long, these guards had to remind people about their badges. The employees had worked there forever and knew the badge protocol but did not seem to care. This frustrated me and I always wanted to yell at them to put their badges on before they got to the gate. It was plain inconsiderate, and I always felt bad for the security guards. I would watch all these employees scowl and grumble at the guards for reminding them to do the right thing. It made no sense to me.

In contrast I would always make a point of smiling and saying, "Good morning!" or "See you on the flip side!"

If they could have, they already would have

Most importantly, I made sure I had my badge on and visible so they could just glance at it and keep the line moving.

I had been working there for two years when we had a huge layoff of 1500 people. They were losing their jobs because we had lost a contract to a competitor. I was assigned to assist people with job searches, resume writing and effective interviewing skills. One evening, after working late, helping folks get ready to transfer to new jobs, I was one of the last people to leave the building. When I got to the security gate, it was just me and the gate guard; all the others had left for the day.

He stopped me and said, "Do you have a minute?"

I said, "Sure, what can I do for you?"

He replied, "I got notified I was laid off today."

I replied, "I am very, very sorry."

"It's okay," he said. "I've already got a new job starting on Monday. I was really hoping to see you before then."

I asked, "Why is that?"

He went on to say, "There are only two people I'm going to miss from here; my supervisor and you."

A little surprised by his statement I said, "Why me?"

If they could have, they already would have

He smiled and said, "Because you always had a smile for us. You were always in a good mood; and you always talked to us like real people." Then he said, "Do you know you've only missed two days of work in the last two years?"

I replied, "I know that; but how do *you* know that?"

He answered, "Because I always looked for your smile to get me through the day, and on those two days I noticed you weren't here."

I said, "Well, I am so happy for you about your new job; good luck on your new career," and I shook his hand and left.

I remember thinking at the time, Wow! Something so insignificant, but it made his day and helped him get through the 7,999 other people who were a bunch of grouches. I had no idea of the impact it had made until that day.

I was glad he took the time to tell me because it made me realize that you have to practice what you preach every day. What you say and how you act, impacts others whether you know it or not.

Another situation occurred at the same place. I had been teaching a communications skills class. One of the things I taught people was to shake hands with their co-workers. I told them that it did not matter if they had been working side-by-side for years; when they walked up to each other

If they could have, they already would have

in the morning, they needed to reach out and shake hands. They should smile at each other and say, "I'm glad you are here today." I told them that shaking hands formed a partnership that said, "We are in this together." It did not matter whether or not they liked that person every day, because if they had been working together for a long time, they probably would have had some conflict between them at some point. Regardless, they were instructed to shake hands. I taught them how to have a firm handshake that says, "You are important and I value you."

Over a four-month period I taught this class to 92 assembly line employees; however, during my normal duties I rarely ran into the assembly line workers.

On one holiday visit my father-in-law asked to see the helicopter production at my company, so I made arrangements for an official tour. The production operated as a multi-station assembly line. An outer shell for the helicopter went into a great big hangar, and after about 20 stations it emerged on the other end as a military attack helicopter. Each station added its component to the helicopter. Our tour started at the first station where five or ten people worked. As we approached and they recognized me, they each walked off their station and came up to shake my hand. This was repeated at every station by every worker. They all walked off the line to shake my hand. It was totally unexpected.

What was supposed to be a 30-minute tour ended up taking two hours! First of all, you do not ever walk off the line in a manufacturing plant, so that was amazing in itself. But

If they could have, they already would have

these people did, and they said things like, "Thank you so much. We come in each day, shake each other's hands and start the day off right. I have re-bonded with the people I've taken for granted for the past 20 years. Now we have forged a 'one team, one fight' attitude toward doing a good job." My father-in-law said, "In my 60 years of work, I have never seen anything like that!" Seeing the positive influence that I had on those people was humbling, to say the least.

Another time, I was crawling into the back of a Super Shuttle van on my way to the airport to catch a very early flight. It was dark outside and I was trying to get settled and ensure I had all my stuff, so I had not noticed the driver.

The driver looked at me through the rear view mirror and in a not-so-friendly voice said, "You don't remember me, do you?"

The tone of voice pricked my senses and I quickly glanced at the driver's card hanging on the dashboard. There I saw the face of a man whom I had fired from his job about a year before. He had been so focused on staying out late and partying that he was unable to perform his job in the morning and ended up fired. *Oh, great,* I thought, *the headlines will read, "Crazed shuttle driver takes final revenge on his tormentor; body found in the desert near the airport."*

I smiled as nicely as I could muster and said, "Hey, yes, I do remember you. How have you been?"

If they could have, they already would have

I saw his eyes flash in the rearview mirror for a second and then his face broke out into a big grin. He said, "Great actually. Getting fired was the best thing that could have happened to me. I didn't know it at the time. It woke me up to what I was doing with my life. I was able to put the parties aside and turn my life around. I am in college now and doing awesome. I drive the shuttle to earn book money. I realized that if you hadn't given me that kick in the ass last year, no telling where I would be by now. I was always hoping I would see you again to say thanks."

As I exhaled the breath I did not even know I was holding I said, "I am so happy with your success and I wish you the best." I left that van smiling, grateful to experience yet another opportunity to see the impact I had had on another--and because I was not going to end up dead in the desert.

One last story: I was doing an investigation for the Army National Guard. One of the witnesses I interviewed said to me, "You know you're being watched, right?"

Puzzled, I asked, "What do you mean?"

He said, "I'm late in getting you my signed statement. But here you are; you're not yelling or screaming. You're making it okay; you're coming to me; you are making it as easy as possible for me to meet your deadline. I'm watching and learning from you because in the past I've been a yeller and screamer. I'm watching you handle it so differently, and get what you need. I wanted you to know you are a wonderful role model. I've been in the military

If they could have, they already would have

almost twenty years and I learned something new from you today."

Once again, it was that opportunity for someone to tell me, "You made a difference in my life today."

As leaders, our lives are an open book. Our actions and our words are on stage for anyone and everyone to see and judge. Be aware that you carry influence, both positive and negative, to all around you. If you are as lucky as I am, you will get to hear the rest of the story about the many ways you have influenced others.

If they could have, they already would have

Chapter 8

Three Campaigns

Wherever I have been assigned or worked, regardless of my new role (worker, first-line supervisor, mid-level manager or senior leader), I bring with me *three campaigns* to that new job site. These campaigns allow me to assess where our organization is currently and helps ensure that the ground level structure is in place. It does not matter the type of job or work involved because these campaigns breach all businesses. These are not assessment tools that are looked at, reviewed and then forgotten. These campaigns are ingrained into the day-to-day fabric of my being; they are not just slogans I stick up on the wall. I attempt to instill them in all of my co-workers, regardless of the hierarchical level.

The campaigns are simple in thought, basic in structure and essential to effectiveness. If everyone buys into these ideas, then you are well on your way to an outstanding organization.

They are:

- Back To Basics,
- Never Walk Past a Mistake, and
- Each One, Teach One.

If they could have, they already would have

Back to Basics

In an organization where people have known each other for ten, fifteen, twenty, even 30 years, everyone gets complacent. You can hear this mindset in casual conversations, "We know our jobs and could do 'em in our sleep." Or, "We are good at what we do and have the history to prove it." They stop telling each other, "You know, you ought to wear your uniform correctly. That name tag is no longer authorized on that jacket." "You ought to read that technical order and not try to do things from memory."

The problem is that things change, such as directives, guidance, and policies; and if we continue to do something the way we have always done it without going back and checking the book, then we are probably missing out and making mistakes.

In the military there is a program called Cross-Tells. It is a way of sharing inspection reports from similar units so you can evaluate your own strengths and weakness based on what was written up in the report on the other unit. I used to view these reports as though they were free ice cream for the kiddies: a non-incriminating way for us to look at others' mistakes or strengths and learn from them. How much better could we be? Many of my co-workers could not see the value in this system. If they did read the report, they simply felt that their programs would never get that bad, but rarely did they check and verify within their own team. They assumed they knew the rules and assumed they knew the true status of their programs. Time

If they could have, they already would have

after time I read about units that failed to implement this or that program being cited from guidance that had been out for months or even years.

So, get *back to basics*! This means to get back to the basics of your job! Regularly read the guidance again; refresh yourself on checklists, read the newsletters; read professional sources. In the military it is beneficial to actually talk to the young Airmen who have recently come out of Basic Training and Technical School and allow them to refresh and update everyone on the basics of their jobs.

Back to Basics focuses on the job and compliance: compliance with technical orders (TOs), Standard Operating Procedures (SOPs), regulations, instructions, laws…all of those written rules that keep us from making the mistakes of the past. Many of those regulations and instructions were written in blood. Someone died because he made a serious mistake.

So find out what those basics are and seek that knowledge! It goes back to "Get in the K+A=R!" Knowledge with a capital K--not "I think," or "I guess," or "I've been doing this for 30 years, therefore, I know the right answer. I don't have to look anything up." Do not make assumptions. Knowledge should be based on being up-to-date on the latest requirements or knowing where to go and look up the answers.

If they could have, they already would have

Rules change every day. Regulations change every year, sometimes every six months, so you have to stay refreshed on the latest guidance.

Take your organization or your five-to-seven employees and get back to the standards. Reset the organization. It does not matter where in the organization you sit…get Back to Basics.

Never Walk Past a Mistake

The people in your organization hail from all walks of life. They have different perspectives and different values. Yet, now they are together in one organization and have to move in the same direction. Many people are not self-policing, however.

Have you taken a vacation cruise lately on one of the mega-ships? With the concerns about communicable viral diseases on these floating cities of 5,000-plus people, cruise liners have a strong "wash your hands" campaign in place. There are signs everywhere instructing you to sanitize your hands before you eat, after you use the facilities, and before you come back on board from being ashore. There are hand-sanitizing stations at the entrance to every restaurant or buffet line. But this is not enough because many people do not use them. The crew post one or two people at each restaurant door with a spray bottle of sanitizer, and they spray the guests' hands before they are allowed to enter. What I observed, the few times the doors were unguarded, was that many people ignored the self-serve wash stations and walked right in. So much for

If they could have, they already would have

people self-policing. If we cannot count on our fellow human beings to take basic safety precautions for our health, what other things are they not doing?

It is essential to establish with your employees the rules of engagement: the boundaries that cover minimum expectations, consequences, and rewards. When I first start a new job, I like to get very basic with my employees and set the expectations, i.e., what I expect from them and what they can expect from me. I have found through trial and error that this needs to be done within the first 30-45 days. If you let unacceptable behavior go unchecked for too long, then the expectation will be that the behavior is acceptable and is the norm. It is okay to sit back and observe for a while before making changes when you first join an organization as long as it pertains to processes or programs, but not when dealing with people's behaviors. Your standards need to be known sooner rather than later.

Here is a sample of the rules of engagement (ROE's) that I use. I provide them in writing to the employees a day before I plan to review them.

The ROE's are:

Use the chain of command. We all know that having more than one boss will drive you nuts. I will work down the chain in the appropriate manner. I will try not to bypass your supervisor to bring something straight to you unless it is an emergency situation. I ask that you do the same. We all owe it to each other, at every level, to respect the positions in the chain. This however, does not prevent

If they could have, they already would have

anyone from jumping the chain if they feel they have a problem they cannot discuss or get resolved at the next higher level.

Keep everyone in the know. It is essential that your supervisor and boss be aware of key items on which you are working. In case of your absence, they can follow up for you. If you think you have something that may result in senior leadership getting a phone call or email, then that is something your supervisor should know so he is prepared if the boss comes asking.

Keep a continuity book. Make a binder, folder or something that shows your key work processes and points of contacts. Make sure it is simple to follow so that someone can cover for you in your absence. Use flowcharts to show your key processes. Explain it to your co-workers or supervisor so that they have a basic understanding of your job requirements.

Ask for help if you need it. We need to help each other at all times. There is too much work and not enough hands in most cases, so teamwork is not optional.

Understand zero tolerance. There is zero tolerance for drug or alcohol abuse, violence or harassment of any kind in this workplace. Treat others as you would like to be treated.

Do your work. If you are paid for eight hours, then work eight hours. Being consistently late to work is not a traffic problem; it is a personal problem that you need to remedy. Excessive breaks, long personal conversations or

If they could have, they already would have

wandering away from your work station for long periods is considered to be theft. It is theft of time. I am not saying that we are not expected to be social in our workplace, but I will let you know when it crosses the line.

Do not gossip! My definition of gossip is talking about someone when he is not present. Gossip undermines the fabric of a team. It is dangerous if left unchecked.

It is important to have a face-to-face conversation with everyone at the same time and go through each of these items. If you distribute these rules for them to read, your level of commitment to the ROE's may not be evident or understood. It is crucial that your workers understand that these are not just nice words; in fact, you plan to hold people accountable for them.

Anytime you walk past a co-worker or employee who is doing something wrong and you do not correct her, you have just trained her that her way of doing business is acceptable. This is where we get to use feedback, the breakfast of champions! This is a *teachable moment*. It is where you teach and course-correct at a moment's notice. It is not about trying to be mean or controlling. It is about keeping everyone inside the boundaries that you have established for performance or behavior. It may deal with whether someone is dressed appropriately in accordance with the standards or whether he is doing his job correctly, or whether he is following the rules about tardiness. Whatever it is, take advantage of the teachable moment. Feedback needs to be immediate and timely. On-the-spot feedback lends itself well to using the BASICS worksheet

161

If they could have, they already would have

we discussed in Chapter 3. It allows you to cover all areas by running the checklist and stating the facts or observations.

B- Behavior - Tell him what you saw him do or say; repeat back to him exactly what he said.

A- Attitude - Explain the problem with the attitude that you saw him display at the time of the mistake, and the attitudes of others observing the mistake.

S- Situation – Remind him of the standard, and explain the difference between what he did and the standard.

I – Impact - Illustrate the impact of why his actions or words were inappropriate; i.e., what were possible safety violations in the situation, or how a bad example was being set.

C- Consequences - Establish the consequences for repeating this behavior. Tell him exactly what will happen; for example, say, "The third time you're late, you will get a Letter of Reprimand and your next promotion will be frozen for six months." Give him a heads-up regarding the consequences. There should be no surprises.

S- Solutions – Ensure he understood what you were saying. If the situation lends itself well to a do-over, then make that happen. The worker will best benefit if he knows where to go from here and what his next steps should be. Involve the employee in rectifying his behavior.

If they could have, they already would have

Create a correction plan which identifies steps and deadlines to eliminate the mistake from happening again.

Now go back to your desk and document this action. Do a Memorandum for Record (MFR); put a little piece of paper, typed or hand-written, in a folder with the employee's name on it. Document that, "On this date I told Airman Jones to get a haircut and he acknowledged understanding of the gap between his appearance and the standard." You need to document this immediately even if you have just said something verbally. If you do not, you will forget about it and get wrapped up in something else. Documenting feedback helps you to see patterns of behavior. It also helps you to acknowledge when people do the right thing after being given feedback.

This documentation is not so you can have proof and catch the person screwing up. It is so you can help the person fix mistakes, grow and develop. If you see a pattern emerging with an individual, you can stop it before it turns into a bigger problem. For example, if an employee is late every Monday or calls in sick every Monday, that is a pattern of behavior. It is also a big clue to underlying issues. This is a pattern of behavior that traditionally indicates alcohol or drug abuse. It means the individual cannot get up and report for duty after a hard-partying weekend. So you are going to want to be able to look back at these patterns of behavior and say, "Wow! Something else might be going on here."

If they could have, they already would have

Never walk past a mistake; give immediate and timely feedback, and document! Remember, if you condone it, you own it. This is a huge part of the supervisor's job.

Each One, Teach One

The campaign I find the most exciting is this one: *Each One, Teach One.* We have so many bright young airmen coming into the military, fresh out of Basic Training and Technical School, and they know the latest stuff. Whenever these young folks join your organization, give them opportunities to share what they have learned, i.e. to teach. Assign them as sponsors, as mentors, assign them to do an in-house training session; give them an hour platform where they can take these crusty old sergeants and give them a refresher on, "This is how we are now doing business. This is the latest information."

Do the same with people returning from conferences, in-residence leadership schools; in fact, any school or training. Give them a chance to teach what they learned. Why? The first reason is that it reinforces what they have learned. Statistics say that seven days after you leave a class, you only remember ten percent of what you heard. Every chance you get to repeat it embeds that learning into your long-term memory. The second reason is that you get the benefit of the multiplier effect of people learning from each other. The easiest way to learn anything is to have to teach it. People pay attention differently in a training environment if they know they are going to have to build their own lesson plans and teach it once they return.

If they could have, they already would have

What this does is to create a learning organization; a growing organization. This creates an organization that does not allow stagnation or regression or only lives in the past.

I recommend that you take all three of these campaigns together:

1. Back to Basics
2. Never Walk Past a Mistake
3. Each One, Teach One

If you do that, you will have an organization that is always re-setting: re-setting back to the latest information. You will see and use 21st Century knowledge that you did not have before. Take that new information, bring it forward, and refresh the organization. Tie that to never walking past a mistake so that people do not slide backwards. If you are giving continuous verbal and documented feedback, you are saying, "No, no, no. Do not slide outside the boundaries. Let's keep moving forward." Then inculcate Each One, Teach One into the organization so that they value teaching and sharing information. In the end you have created a learning organization, a cutting edge organization. You become an organization that sets the standards for others.

If you want to be a showcase unit, and if you want to build a culture of greatness, you are going to have to inculcate these three campaigns, and it has to happen at every level, from airmen to generals (in the military) or from worker to CEO (in a civilian company).

If they could have, they already would have

Your organizational culture has to be one that is willing to take feedback and value it. You have to reward a young airman who sees a Lt Colonel wearing his hat incorrectly and takes action to correct it. They should feel comfortable saying, "Sir/Ma'am: That's inappropriate." The colonel needs to have been trained to reply, "Thank you, Airman; I appreciate that feedback!" then press on, and not get defensive about the feedback. Take the opportunity to set the standard that it is okay to give respectful, tactful feedback, regardless of the rank or position of the person. The mindset should be that everyone is looking out for each other.

Take these three campaigns and establish an organizational culture that says, "We are going to be on the cutting edge of the future, not resting on our laurels of the past."

If they could have, they already would have

Chapter 9

Leaders as Problem Solvers

There are tangible skills that a great leader needs in their toolbox. Once a leader understands the mission or purpose of the organization, he must establish the vision for the people. Next, the leader conducts a self-assessment to determine the status of the organization's ability to achieve the mission/purpose. If there are gaps between the current state and the desired state (i.e. the envisioned future), then the leader must implement problem solving systems throughout the organization.

Give people the tools to solve problems! There are many problem-solving tools available. Here is one that has evolved from four decades of solving problems in manufacturing, academia, training and development, the service industry, administrative environments, civil service (government agencies), and all military agencies. I call it the "SOLVE IT!" model. The acronym makes it easy to remember the systematic steps involved in effective problem solving.

To build an outstanding organization, it is vital to institutionalize a systematic approach to problem solving among all employees at all levels. Then reward and recognize those successes. True organizational success comes from empowering people to innovate at their level from wherever they sit in the organization.

If they could have, they already would have

SOLVE IT

(7-Step Problem Solving Model)

S   **S**tate the problem

O   **O**rganize efforts

L   **L**ist root causes

V   **V**erify solutions

E   **E**xecute!

I   **I**nstitutionalize results

T   **T**rain Employees

1. State the problem. Confirm that there is a problem. A problem exists when there is a gap between the current state and the desired (envisioned) state. If there is no gap, there is no problem. This is the most important step: start with a clearly defined problem. If not, employees will find themselves chasing symptoms instead of solutions.

The problem statement looks like this:

As is state:_____ vs. Desired state:_____

Example: There is a 49% efficiency rate vs. a desired 95% efficiency rate on Line 6 (in a manufacturing plant.) Is there a gap? Yes. There is a 46% efficiency deficit. This problem is worth expending the time, energy, labor,

If they could have, they already would have

and money to explore with a problem-solving team. If the data revealed that there was a 96% efficiency rate on Line 6, there would not be a problem. The team should identify another problem to solve.

An effective and simple technique to identify problems is to ask employees who work inside the process, *"If you could change one thing, what would you change?"* Let them brainstorm a list of these items, and then prioritize those items. Start with problems that have a quick fix. Get those quick successes under their belt to build their confidence in themselves and their problem solving skills. They are also building their confidence in leadership support. Once, you as their leader, celebrate their efforts, they will realize you are serious about letting them solve problems. This is tangible evidence that you are invested in their success and in running an outstanding organization.

Once employees have identified a topic to study, they will have to collect some initial data to confirm the 'gap' between the current state and the desired state. They may find they do not have a problem. It could be an irritant. At that point, they should move to their second topic and collect data to confirm the problem exists.

In some cases, the fixes do not require a huge team effort to solve. Some fixes just need to be done; we call these DIN's … i.e. do it now! For example, if an appointment letter is missing, then create, sign, and file the appointment letter. It does not take a committee to fix it.

If they could have, they already would have

The leader's job is to filter through the list of problems and determine if the effort needs a single person given authority to fix it or to assign a cross-functional team with a trained facilitator.

2. Organize efforts. Once the problem is confirmed and a team is assigned to solve it, it is time to get organized. During this step, the team will do the following:

    a. Identify team members required to solve the problem.
    b. Set short and long-term goals for process improvement.
    c. Flowchart the 'as is' process (walk through the steps).
    d. Develop a data collection plan (who, where, what type, how often).
    e. Gather data at identified steps in the process.
    f. Identify the resources needed to study the problem.
    g. Identify subject matter experts that may need to weigh in.

Many teams make the mistake of rushing to identify solutions before doing this foundational and critical work. This work can be tedious and team members will be chomping at the bit to move to solutions. It is imperative that the leader values this step and the behind-the-scenes work required at this stage. Ensure there are periodic

If they could have, they already would have

briefings by the team in front of leaders during this stage so the employees know these steps are important.

3. List Root Causes. Once initial data is collected and the 'as is' process is understood and mapped, the team can look for the root causes of the problem. If the root causes are not clearly identified, the team will aim solutions at symptoms. This will be wasted effort and time. Teams should spend most of their time on this step. It is as important as validating the problem in step 1. The solutions should jump right out when root causes are confirmed. The team will use root cause analysis (RCA) tools to identify topics and data to explore.

  a. Brainstorm causes
  b. Fishbone diagrams
  c. Affinity diagrams
  d. Run charts
  e. Statistical Process Control (SPC) charts
  f. Check sheets
  g. Pareto charts
  h. Flowcharting
  i. Timing analysis
  j. Skills analysis

These tools are helpful for various processes. A trained facilitator will help identify the most applicable tool and take the team through the implementation steps for each one. The team can also Google these tools and walk through the steps. The SPC charts are the most

If they could have, they already would have

sophisticated tools listed above, and require additional subject matter expertise. They are also the most predictive, which is powerful when looking for root causes and solutions.

4. Verify solutions. The team will take the following steps after the root causes are confirmed:

   a. Brainstorm solutions; prioritize top 3 recommended solutions.
   b. Conduct cost/benefit analyses on each proposed solution.
   c. Present options to Leadership Team/First Line Supervisor.
   d. Leadership Team picks one to implement or offers an alternative solution.
   e. Develop implementation plan:
      1. Who is going to do what by when?
      2. Gather execution team. Everyone who touches the process should be on the execution team. These individuals may not have been on the problem solving team, but will need to have buy-in to the solution.

If they could have, they already would have

5. Execute! It is now time to execute the chosen solution.
- a. Execute the implementation plan formulated in Step 4.
- b. Take careful notes and collect data at every stage in the implementation process.
- c. Compare the 'desired state' to the new 'as is' state (after executing the solution).
- d. There are only three possible outcomes once a solution has been implemented:
  1. Did the process get better?
  2. Did the process get worse?
  3. Did the process stay the same?
- e. Document the results using before-and-after charts or narrative descriptions.
- f. Prepare presentation of results.
- g. Present solutions, results, and analysis to Leadership Team.

6. Institutionalize results:
- a. Build checklists, procedures, continuity binders, training manuals, employee handbooks to hold the gains. This is one of the most over-looked steps. It is common for everything to reset back to the old way of doing business and lose all the gains from the problem-solving team's efforts. The leader must follow up with the team and process owners

If they could have, they already would have

      to ensure they have institutionalized the solutions into policies, procedures, checklists, and manuals. Rewarding the employees who execute the new solution is also effective to sustain the progress.
- b. If the process got worse or stayed the same, undo the solution, execute another solution, and check the new results for improvement.

7. Train employees:

    a. Train all current and new employees on the new procedures, processes, and policies.
    b. Ensure replacement employees are also trained on results of problem-solving efforts.
    c. Incorporate new processes, practices, and policies into the organization's culture.
    d. Keep leadership informed of any new developments or unintended consequences.

Real World Applications:

At a manufacturing organization in Midwest America, a new plant manager used this 7-step problem-solving technique which revealed that a piece of equipment had been installed backwards 15 years earlier. The Manager jump-started the process when he asked the long-term employees, "If you could change one thing, what would you change?" One person stated, "This equipment in the middle of the manufacturing process has been

If they could have, they already would have

backwards since it was installed 15 years ago and it slows us down. I would turn it around." To do that would be mean to shut down production for two days. If you know the manufacturing world, you know this is just not done!

The new manager tasked the team to see what it would take to turn it around. A team of subject matter experts and process owners was formed. The team spent an hour a day planning (i.e. organizing their efforts), and identified the steps it would take to turn the machine around in minimum time. The team confirmed that the greatest wasted production time occurred at the 'backwards' machine (i.e. it was the root cause). Specifically, four people had to pick up a piece of molded steel and walk it around to the 'front' end of the machine so that it could be placed on the next piece of equipment for additional bending. Then they had to pick up the molded steel and carry it from the 'back' end of the machine to the next station.

As the consultant to the project, I coached the manager that he could not lay people off on the two days of shutdown. That would send the wrong signal to the rest of the manufacturing members that problem solving would 'cost them' in their paycheck. Finally, the team was ready to shut down the production line and turn the machine around. This huge piece of equipment required 10 people and a forklift to move. The 70 other plant employees surrounded the area to watch. Then an amazing and totally unexpected phenomenon occurred.

If they could have, they already would have

As the ten people began to work on unbolting the machine from the cement floor, the observers began to anticipate their needs and handed them tools without a word spoken. They come forward and helped balance the machine on four sides, once again without a word spoken. A process predicted to take two days took less than one day.

After the rotation of the equipment, the line improved by 37 percent! The employees more than made up for the one day of down time. Most importantly, the entire workforce was invested in the team's success. If 70 people had been laid off, even for one day, the impact on employee morale and dedication to problem solving would have been catastrophic. The manager would have gained ten problem-solvers and lost 70! It was a tough business decision for the new manager to make. The leader had to trust the problem solving process and acknowledge that, in this case, observers were part of the problem solving team.

The next example of applied problem solving occurred at a military medical unit. The unit provided annual physical assessments for 1,200 personnel. The national goal was 82 percent of all military members must have a current annual physical. This unit's rate was 49 percent.

Problem statement: The annual physical exam percentage rate is 49 percent versus the national standard of 82 percent. Was there a gap? Yes! A team of people comprised of lab technicians, medics, nurses, and doctors

If they could have, they already would have

was assembled. The team organized their efforts and collected initial data at the major steps in the physical exam process. Not only was the physical exam percentage 33 points too low, the process was averaging eight hours per person. One of the root causes for the low unit percentage was because supervisors could not afford to lose their members for an entire day. The team flowcharted the process and began to collect real-time data about how long each step in the process was taking (check-in and out, lab draws, immunizations, vital signs, optometry, doctor visit, and quality control on the records). Significant wait times were recorded at check-in and check-out, as well as labs and immunizations. These were the root causes.

The team recommended reallocating and training additional personnel to these sections. Administrative assistants took over control of the check in and out stages so that medics could be allocated to labs and immunizations. In addition, public health and biomedical equipment repairmen were used as facilitators to move people from long lines to shorter lines, thereby, moving through quickly. A trained senior medic was assigned to conduct the QC on the medical records. The team also recommended a "by appointment" process that reduced the number of people present in the clinic at any given time.

The bottom line, after executing these solutions, was that the average time for a physical exam was reduced from eight hours to one-to-two hours. After three consistent

If they could have, they already would have

months at these rates, the medical commander was able to go to the other commanders and assure them that, if they would send their people, the maximum 'lost' time would be no more than two hours. The other commanders were willing to try it. The new process was institutionalized in checklists. All incoming new members were trained on their roles, responsibilities, and assignments during the physical exam process. The gains have been sustained for over five years as of 2016. The unit physical exam percentage rating went from an average of 49 percent to a sustained average of 85 percent in that time. In fact, the team went from being rated number 93 out of 93 medical units to being in the top 10 medical units in the country.

Problem solving takes time, labor, money, and commitment on the part of leadership and the employees who work inside the processes and programs. Problem solving is a key leadership skill. It must be perceived as an investment. Once a leader accepts problem solving as a key leadership skill, the results are immediate.

Problem solving is a multiplier effect. It is a structured and 'safe' way to involve employees in the strategies and goals of the organization. By training people in problem solving, the leader can offer individualized and team consideration, set challenging goals, and motivation, rewards, and recognition (all key components of a transformational leader). By setting the example as a problem solver, the leader empowers employees to take risks using a systematic approach.

Leadership must be involved at several stages in the problem solving process. By receiving regular reports from the teams, the leader gives top-cover and reassurance to the team that what they are doing is important and valued. Building a problem solving culture is a tangible and structured avenue toward building an outstanding organization. And as noted before, outstanding attracts outstanding.

Chapter 10

Get Up, Suit Up, and Show Up!

Finally, the single most important lesson I have to offer has to do with dealing with the sucker punches of life. You know what those are; those tragic things that happen and take you to your knees. I experienced several significant sucker punches in my life. I call them the "Big 4."

1. My father shot and killed my mother when I was 18.
2. I was in a very bad car accident and almost died in 1994; the lady in the other car did die, and I was at fault.
3. My seventeen-year-old son died in my arms two years later from injuries in a car accident.
4. I was told I had cancer with no known cause and no known cure.

When the sucker punches of life knock you to your knees, there is only one thing left to do: *Get up, suit up, and show up*, every day, to life!

When you want to pull the covers over your head because you are in so much pain, get up, suit up and show up. Do it when you want to scream at the top of your lungs, "Go away, cruel world, I have done my time!" Do it when you want to call in sick and tired. And when you are in the most pain of your life, but you crawl out of bed, drag yourself to the closet, grab some clothes, throw yourself together and drag yourself to work … that is VICTORY!

If they could have, they already would have

If on that same day, instead of sitting there and staring at a computer screen, you also train, trust, serve, love, learn or lead, that is SUCCESS! Success is not about big houses, lots of money or fancy cars. When you die, you cannot take your stuff with you.

So I challenge you to serve something greater than yourself each day. Whether you are showing up to work, or volunteering at the local community center or your child's school, or being a great parent and bringing up your children to be great citizens, get up, suit up, and show up to life.

If they could have, they already would have

Epilogue

Final Lesson: The Show Must go On!

Jolene: As consultants to a large manufacturing and distribution company, Paula and I were teaching a class in Dallas, Texas for front-line employees. It was a two-day program held in a local hotel. We were staying at the hotel and using their conference rooms for the training. Our students lived locally and came in daily for the classes. Early the second day, at about 6:00 a.m., we were blasted awake by the blaring horns of the hotel fire alarms.

In a true military fashion, our training kicked in and we evacuated our third-floor rooms in a matter of seconds. We rushed down the back stairwell to the long grassy lawn behind the hotel. It was winter, so it was dark, wet and cold when we exited. We moved away from the building and took stock of our belongings. Paula had thrown on her raincoat over her nightclothes and put on her high-heeled shoes. In her pockets she found a tube of lipstick, a tissue, and a stick of gum. I had thrown the thick terry cloth bathrobe over my pajamas and had put on my shoes as well. In my pocket I found my cigarettes and a lighter and nothing else.

Soon we heard the first responder sirens and started seeing other residents exit the hotel. We did not feel quite as vulnerable about our attire when we saw one gentleman

If they could have, they already would have

dressed only in a bath towel and cowboy hat go sauntering by.

Eventually we made our way around to the front of the hotel and saw the firemen in full swing swarming the building. By now our feet were drenched from the wet grass and the cold had settled into our bones.

As the sun was coming up and we were still holding vigil at the side of the building, shivering, it dawned on us that our students would soon be arriving for class, see the commotion with the fire trucks and worry about our well-being. We started scanning the crowd and finally located two of our students. With the assistance of a passerby, we got their attention and flagged them to come over to our hideout. The news media had arrived and after finishing interviewing the more colorfully dressed residents, they were on patrol looking for more victims to share their story. We wanted nothing to do with getting our fifteen minutes of fame on the nightly news, and much preferred our secluded location. When our two students arrived it was obvious by the look on their faces that we looked a mess. Even Paula's recently applied lipstick could not cover up the unkempt, frozen appearance that we both portrayed.

As we filled them in on the nocturnal events, I could not help but notice that both Paula's and my eyes kept drifting down to look at their warm, dry socks. Paula finally blurted out what was obviously on both of our frozen minds, "Can we borrow your socks?"

If they could have, they already would have

The guys stared at each other for a split second too long, obviously thinking we were crazy, but they finally agreed to hand over their long white tube socks. We were grinning ear-to-ear when the warmth of the socks started to ease our frozen feet. The guys then set off to locate the rest of the students and find out from the hotel staff what the prognosis was for us to return to our hotel rooms.

They returned eventually, with all our students in tow and instructions from the hotel staff that we could not go back in. We were set up in a conference room in the office building next door, however. This building had become an impromptu holding area for the dislocated guests.

We were shown to our conference room. At that point we had to decide if we were going to conduct the training or wait until we were able to move back into the hotel training room. But as you know, the show must go on.

Paula: I can only guess how hard it was for our students to maintain their straight faces as we stood in front of the class, teaching in our pajamas. When Jolene got up to go to the bathroom, none of us could handle it any longer. We burst into laughter and could not stop laughing for ten full minutes. We were crying and falling out of our chairs.

Jolene again: During a break I made my way down the office hallway in search of the ladies' room. As I passed a desk I overheard one woman say to her co-worker, "If I looked like that, I would be so embarrassed." I turned to them and said, "I am!" and kept walking. Upon entering the ladies' room and seeing my reflection in the mirror, I

If they could have, they already would have

burst out laughing. My PJs were an old-fashioned flannel night shirt like the type Ebenezer Scrooge wore. Not only was it the oldest, most unfashionable attire I could have been wearing, I now noticed that it was on inside out and the seams were showing. Add to that the bare legs above the white tube socks pulled up to my knees, topped off with my black dress shoes, I was a sorry sight. At least Paula was wearing nice-looking hot pink flannel PJs and her candy apple red raincoat covered her down to her calves. Somehow the tube socks looked more stylish on her with her high-heeled shoes.

It was almost noon before we were allowed back into our rooms and transformed ourselves into our normal professional consultant selves.

After this trip, Paula bought me silk lounging PJs as a present for future trips. We washed the socks and mailed them back to their owners with a thank-you note tucked inside. We were ultimately proud of ourselves that the mission was accomplished regardless of a little hotel fire thrown into our paths. We got up, suited up and showed up.

Two years later, the assessment cycle brought us back to Dallas to train the next round of interviewers. As the students arrived, each of them brought a pair of tube socks and presented them to us. They said, "We are not sure why we had to bring these but we were told to do so and that you two would explain."

If they could have, they already would have

COLONEL (RET) PAULA F. PENSON

Colonel (Ret) Paula Francies Penson has resumed her position as President, *Francies West, LLC*, an organizational and leadership development corporation, after serving in support of the on-going Global War on Terrorism since 9/11/2001. Her business organization consults on: Leadership Training and Development, Team Building, MBTI administration, Program Management, Process and Quality Control, Problem Solving, BASICS of Feedback, and conducts Organizational and Climate Assessments. Francies West was incorporated in 1997.

Col Penson's civilian career paralleled her military assignments with civil service positions in the Department of the Navy, the Army National Guard (National Guard Bureau) and Congressional Affairs for U.S. Southern Command (SOUTHCOM) (joint assignment). Her civilian career experience includes Faculty Associate, Arizona State University; Faculty, Maricopa County Community Colleges; Organizational Development (OD) Manager for McDonnell Douglas Helicopter Company; First Line Supervisor, Ozarka Water Company and OD Consultant to Perrier Group of America, and President of her own consulting company, Francies West, LLC.

EDUCATION
Pursuing, EdD, Organizational Leadership; Grand Canyon University, AZ
1987 M.A. Organizational Communication, Arizona State, Tempe, AZ
1983 B.S. Communication, Arizona State University, Tempe, AZ
1983 AAS, Administration, CCAF, Maxwell AFB, AL

AWARDS & DECORATIONS
Legion of Merit; Meritorious Service Medal (4); AF Commendation Medal (2); Army Commendation Medal; AF Achievement Medal; Army Achievement Medal; AF Outstanding Unit Award (5); Army Superior Unit Award; National Defense Service Medal (3); Global War on Terrorism; Outstanding Teacher, 1984, Arizona State University

If they could have, they already would have

CMSgt (RET) JOLENE R. MEYER

Command Chief Master Sergeant (Ret) Jolene Meyer was born in Rock Island, Illinois in December 1957. She graduated from John F. Kennedy High School, in Cedar Rapids, Iowa and went on to receive her Nursing Degree from St. Luke's College in 1977. CMSgt Meyer entered the Air Force in October 1978. In the first part of her career her areas of expertise involved nuclear, chemical and biological warfare and emergency management. The latter part of her career was focused on organizational development and financial management. CMSgt Meyer is a recognized expert in cultural assessment and leadership enrichment. Her assignments included bases in Arizona, California, Colorado, Hawaii, Virginia, Texas and United Kingdom. She spent twelve years with an F-16 Fighter Wing where she held positions in several squadrons and groups. In her last appointment, as Command Chief Master Sergeant, she served as the senior enlisted advisor and was the liaison between the enlisted and officer core. CMSgt Meyer retired from the military in 1999 and later entered the federal civil service where she served as the Financial and Compliance Program Manager at the 624th Reserve Group at Hickam AFB, HI and the Air Force Petroleum Agency at Ft Belvoir ,VA. She retired after 30 years of combined federal service to join her husband, Mike and their two Yorkshire terriers in Deming, New Mexico. She is currently the Vice President of Francis West, LLC and has consulted for such organizations as Perrier Group of America, Princess Hotels, Siemens Electronics and Maricopa County Department of Transportation.

EDUCATION

1977 AAS, Practical Nursing; St Luke's School of Nursing, Cedar Rapids, IA
1988 AAS, Disaster Preparedness Technology, Lowry AFB, CO (Distinguished Graduate)
1994 Certified Emergency Manager, National Coordinating Council on Emergency Management
2012 Certified Federal Financial Manager

AWARDS AND DECORATIONS

Air Force Meritorious Service Medal (2); Air Force Meritorious Civilian Service Medal; Air Force Commendation Medal (4); Air Force Achievement Medal (2); Air Force Outstanding Unit Award (4); 1985 US Forces in Europe Disaster Preparedness NCO of the Year; 1986 US Forces in Europe Disaster Preparedness NCO of the Year; 1986 US Air Force NCO of the Year (Runner Up)

If they could have, they already would have

> **Motivational speaking and training classes**
>
> Contact *Francies West, LLC* at:
>
> francieswest@consultant.com

- **BASICS©** of Feedback Training Sessions
- Climate Surveys and Customized Debriefings
- Continuous Process Improvement (CPI) Training
- CPI Team Facilitation
- Customer Service Climate Surveys
- Executive and Senior Leader Training
- First Line Supervisor Training: **Surface the SHIPS!**
- Leadership Training and Development
- Middle Management Leadership Training
- Motivational Speaking Engagements: **BE STILL!**
- Myers Briggs Type Indicator (MBTI) Trainer
- Problem Solving Model Training **(SOLVE IT!©)**
- Train-the-Trainer - **(SOLVE IT!©)**
- Program Management 101 Training
- Process and Quality Control Assessment
- Organizational Assessments
- Organizational Culture Assessments
- Team Building Exercises and Facilitation
- Train-the-Trainer Customized Development

Made in the USA
Columbia, SC
13 January 2020